The Myth of Genesis and Exodus and the Exclusion of Their African Origins

THE BLACK MAN'S RELIGION

VOLUME II

The Myth of Genesis and Exodus and the Exclusion of Their African Origins

Yosef ben-Jochannan

Black Classic Press
Baltimore, MD

The Myth of Genesis and Exodus and the Exclusion of Their African Origins

Published by Alkebu-Ian Book Associates 1974
Published by Black Classic Press 2002

Library of Congress Card Catalog Number: 96-83454

ISBN 0-933121-76-8

Cover art by Tony Browder, rendered from the original cover design by Yosef ben-Jochannan

Front Cover: The Sun-GOD-Ra; the Ever-Seeing Eye-GOD-Horus; the House of Fire-Pyramid; the Golden Rooster-GOD-Damballah Ouedo and Voodum; the Ankh-original KEY OF LIFE-or Christian Cross of late; the DOG STAR or later Jewish Star of David; the GRAMADON of ancient times, or reverse German Swastika; the CRESCENT STAR or present Moslem Crescent of modern times; 1–11BASIC MASONIFIED NUMEROLOGY of Mysteries Sytem.

Founded in 1978, Black Classic Press specializes in bringing to light obscure and significant works by and about people of African descent. If our books are not available in your area, ask your local bookseller to order them. Our current list of titles can be obtained by writing:

Black Classic Press
c/o List
P.O. Box 13414
Baltimore, MD 21203

CREDIT:

It is virtually impossible to produce a work of this dimension without the assistance of others. Thus I have to give credit to the following people for their voluntary contributions before and after the final manuscript was completed.

To the Reverends George P. Polk, William F. Hawkins, James E. Gunther and Rabbi Hailu Paris I am most indebted for their constant insistance that I complete the extended documentation of the role of the African [BLACK] People in the creation and development of religion promised in Volume I - AFRICAN ORIGINS OF THE MAJOR "WESTERN RELIGIONS." Along with these men was my daughter - Collette Makeda - in her insistance that I show the manner in which the female's role in the theosophy and theology was distorted, particularly in the "Adam and Eve in the Garden of Eden" syndrome written in the "Holy Bible's OLD TESTAMENT.

To the many African students at the International House, 500 Riverside Drive, New York City, New York; students at Malcolm-King College, Harlem, New York City, New York; and students at Cornell University's Africana Institute And Research Center, Ithaca, New York; I owe much for their encouragement in presenting the completed in two phases: [1] The three volumes under one cover as a "Collector's Item." [2] The separation of each volume under separate cover.

As usual it is to the noted scholar, historian, researcher and professor George E. Simmonds - the President of Alkebu-lan Books Associates and Visiting Professor of History at Malcolm-King College, that I am the most indebted. Without his editing and checking the historical documents, illustrations, dates, events, etc. throughout the entire text of the three volumes I would not have had the type of professional verification necessary in this type of scholarship. It is also Professor Simmonds I had to rely upon to assist me in making the end result meet the very meager budget I had in order to produce this work. Of course my printers - Charley and Richie of A.B.C. Printers, Yonkers, New York must share in the latter credit for their guidance in making the budget fit their outline for production.

The encouragement by the officers and members of Alkebu-lan Foundation, Inc., the parent body of Alkebu-lan Books Associates, along with a friend of the Foundation - Mr. Lloyd Dickens - who gave a "Grant" towards the printing of the volumes, was without any doubt very much instrumental in making the finish product as reasonable as it is in price. But most of all; I am totally indebted to my friends and family that believe in me explicitly.

OTHER WORKS BY THE AUTHOR, AND WITH CO-AUTHORS:

We The Black Jews [Spanish pamphlet, 1949]

The Rape Of Africa And The Crisis In Angola [Ghana, 1958]

An African Nationalist View Of Black Power [New York CORE, pamphlet, 1966]

Africa: The Land, The People, The Culture [co-authors: Y. ben-Jochannan, Ph.D., K. Webb, Ph.D., H. Brooks, Ph. D., W.H. Sadlier Company, New York, N.Y., 1969]

Southern Lands [Ibid]

Southern Neighbours [Ibid]

Arab World, New Africa [Ibid, consultant]

Black Man Of The Nile [Ist Edition 1970, to 5th impression], Alkebu-lan Books Associates, New York, N.Y., 1971

African Origins Of The Major "Western Religions," [same publisher, 1970]

Africa: Mother Of "Western Civilization" [same publisher, 1971]

The Black Man's North And East Africa [same publisher, co-authors: Y. ben-Jochannan and G.E. Simmonds, 1971]

Black Man Of The Nile And His Family [same publisher, 1972]

Cultural Genocide In The Black And African Studies Curriculum [same publisher, 1973]

A Chronology Of The Bible: Challenge To The Standard Version [same publisher, 1973]

The Need For A Holy Black Bible, Vol. III [same publisher, 1974]

Extracts and Comments From The Holy Black Bible [same publisher, 1974]

AFRICAN-AMERICAN HERITAGE SERIES PUBLICATIONS BY THE AUTHOR TO BE RELEASED IN THE VERY NEAR FUTURE, PRESENTLY BEING EDITED:

Another Aspect of Pan-Africanism

Africa And Her Ever-Changing Maps

Africa [Alkebu-lan] In History: A Chronology, 1,750,000 B.C.E. to 1972 C.E.

Front cover: "Gods and Goddesses of the Egyption Religion." Rear cover: Scene from "The Weighing Of The Scribe Ani's Heart" in the Book Of The Coming Forth By Day And By Night. Designed by Yosef ben-Jochannan;

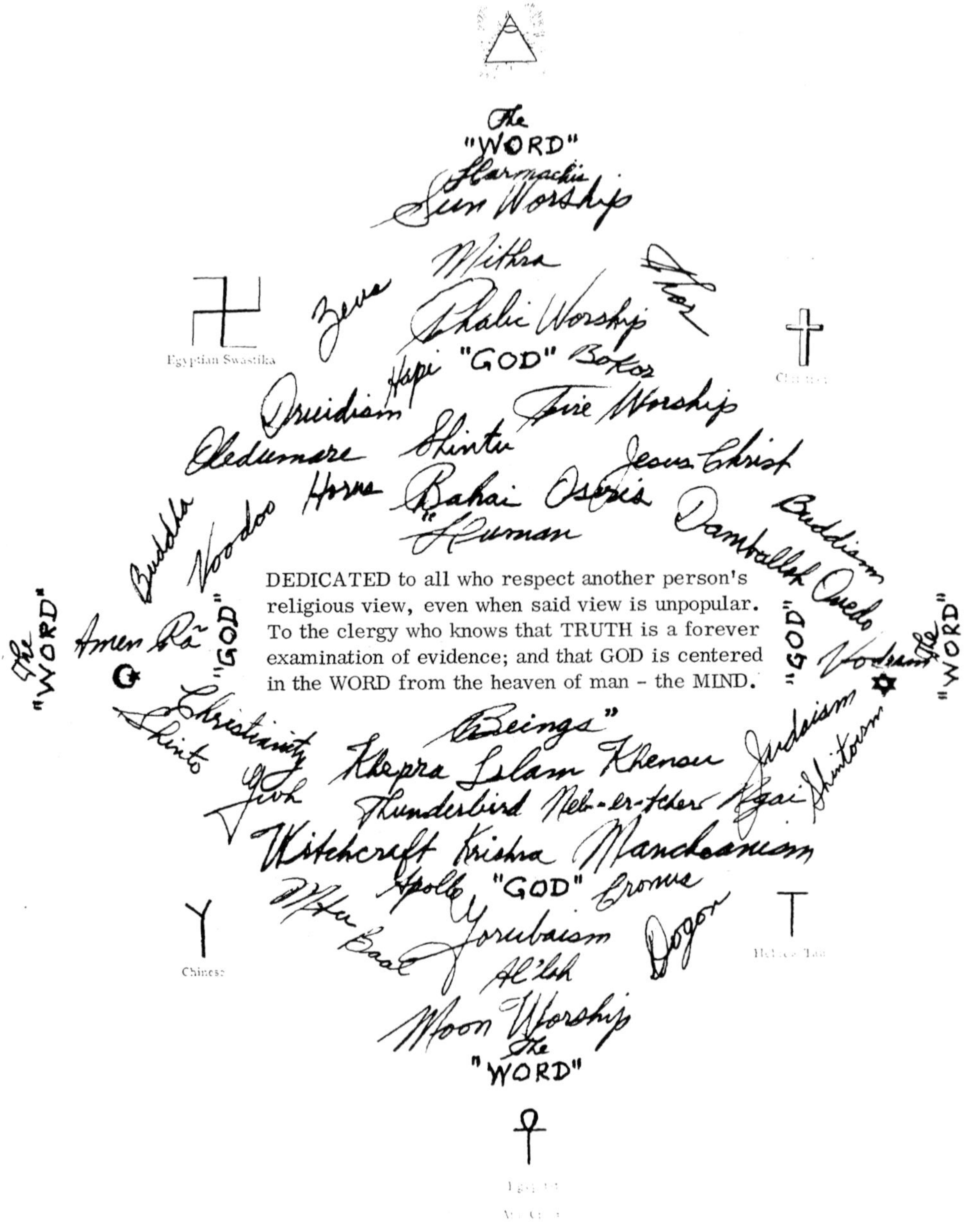

DEDICATED to all who respect another person's religious view, even when said view is unpopular. To the clergy who knows that TRUTH is a forever examination of evidence; and that GOD is centered in the WORD from the heaven of man - the MIND.

CHRONOLOGY OF THE OFFERINGS

ILLUSTRATIONS : For Lecture No. I

ILLUSTRATIONS : For Lecture No. II

---

1. All of the maps are detailed from the stories related to them in the BOOK OF THE DEAD and/or the FIVE BOOKS OF MOSES [Holy Torah or Old Testament]. The exact location or boundaries of each nation is speculative and approximate.

PRELUDE TO GENESIS

As we contemptuously continue looking at Africa and African people through European and European-American eyes and values the Egyptians and their fellow North African neighbours must remain "LILY-WHITE SEMITES." Thus what I am embarking upon here must encounter the same type of Jewish, Christian and Islamic religious bigotry and Caucasian-Semitic [WHITE] racism by those whose sacred interest in this area I have disturbed before, and would have damaged again before the end of this Lecture. For there is no real desire by the so-called "RELIGIOUS," as it appears to me, to allow"... THE TRUTH SHALL SET YOU FREE...prove itself in the face of evidence to the contrary of the current teachings on biblical mythology and the so-called "GREEK ORIGIN OF WESTERN CIVILIZATION." This you will readily observe, when I dare to challenge the sacred domain of the "GOD INSPIRED SCRIBES" of the "CHOSEN PEOPLE," who allegedly wrote down the "WORDS" dictated to them by the Jewish [or Israelite] God - JEHOVAH - himself; equally when I confront the tabooed holy circle of the origin of a "PURE WHITE" color Caucasian and Semitic tradition of something called "GREEK PHILOSOPHY" in each and every white-controlled institution in the "Western World." But I beg to remind you that the term..."WHITE-CONTROLLED"...equally applies to the so-called "NEGRO" and "COLORED-OWNED INSTITUTIONS" - where the same interpretations of a "WHITE" Judaism, Christianity and "GREEK" philosophy are being taught without the slightest bit of examination of the evidence being presented to the African-American victims of such white racism and Judaeo-Christian-Islamic bigotry...THE BLACK STUDENTS. Yet I am convinced by my own studies and experiences, beginning in 1936 C.E. to this present day, that the main challenge to every BLACK EDUCATOR in the "Western World" is in the field of religious history; that dealing with the origin and teachings of Judaism, Christianity and Islam; particularly the damage they have already caused African people everywhere, and will yet cause if not properly re-examined and re-revised. The same appraisal holds true for so-called "Greek Philosophy." For there could be no physical revolution or cultural revolution by any group under the control of their slavemaster until they can free their own minds from their slavemaster's religion and philosophy of superiority...irrespective of the slavemaster's educational insitutions and academicians that establish the slave's frame of reference of "TRUTH" and "AUTHORITY."

In many of the books I have written, such as AFRICAN ORIGINS OF THE MAJOR

"WESTERN RELIGIONS": Judaism, Christianity and Islam; AFRICA: MOTHER OF "WESTERN CIVILIZATION;" and BLACK MAN OF THE NILE [also the revised and enlarged version]...BLACK MAN OF THE NILE AND HIS FAMILY ; I have purposely emphasized the histo-political and socio-religious relationship of the African-Asian-European peoples of the ancient biblical traditions of the overall geography that formed their "WORLD," upon which their ancient dramas were performed; all with a particular emphasis on the African origin in practically everyone of the dramatic scenes. In this Volume , on the other hand, it is with the RELIGIOUS and PHILOSOPHICAL African genesis of so-called "WHITE" and/or "SEMITIC" Judaeo-Christian-Islamic "HOLY WRITINGS" on "THE CREATION OF THE WORLD," also the Greek plagiarization of the Africans of the Nile Valley MYSTERIES SYSTEM'S works...much of which were later on called "GREEK PHILOSOPHY," that I am mainly concerned. The reason for this concern should be obvious; if not, it is because those who are not knowledgeable have never truly studied the Jewish, Christian and/or Moslem "HOLY BIBLE"....respectively called Torah, New Testament and Quran.

This task is not welcome, in the sense that I am taking an unpopular stand against the teachings which my parents and other loveones taught me...believing that they were imparting...

"THE ONLY TRUTH THERE IS ABOUT HOW MANKIND ORIGINATED"...;

a statement I seem to be able to hear my dearly beloved mother still reminding me, as if she was living today. But, they were quite innocent of any wrongdoing for so teaching me, though they were in error of the facts, since they did not know of the existing evidence and facts quite to the contrary. It is certainly those who knew better - rabbis, priests, ministers, theologians and countless others who have taken it upon themselves to speak in the name of their respective God-head [Jehovah, Jesus Christ or Al'lah, etc.] had equally, for sometime during my youth, steered me down the same 'blind alley' of total RELIGIOUS BIGOTRY and RACIAL PREJUDICE against my own self and my indigenous African traditions and heritage, in preference for my imposed European and European-American [WHITE WESTERN] civilization;" all of this inspite of the fact that even in the so-called "Sacred Writings Of God"[1] the setting of God's dramas always included Africa's[2] Punt, Kush [or Ethiopia], Nubia , Meröe and Egypt.

---

1. Jewish "YWH;" Christian "JESUS CHRIST;" and Moslem "AL'LAH."
2. See page xxvi of BLACK MAN OF THE NILE AND HIS FAMILY. This continent was called ALKEBU-LAN by its indigenous people before the Greeks renamed it "AFRIKA" or "AFRICA."

For it was there, along the banks of the Nile River [BLUE and WHITE],[1] the Atbara River[2] and the Great Lakes[3] of Africa, also along the banks of Asia's Tigris and Euphrates River, that said interplay and amalgamation of mankind's GENESIS stories were created and developed - TRUTHS, HALF-TRUTHS, LIES, MYTHS, ALLEGORIES and DISTORTIONS - of the alleged "BIBLICAL FACTS" we, today, still rely upon for our total ...

"SALVATION IN THE NEXT WORLD TO COME."

But the irony of it all is that the people - EUROPEANS - who now claim sole origin of said experience, at the exclusion of one of the continents and its people - AFRICA and AFRICANS, and of the principals who started it all - the indigenous AFRICANS, after having enslaved their African and Asian teachers, still find it impossible to recognize the AFRICAN ORIGIN OF JUDAISM, CHRISTIANITY and ISLAM. Why? Due to the BLACK color of the Africans - the co-originators of the JUDAEO-CHRISTIAN-ISLAMIC GENESIS, this being true only over the last two hundred years. Certainly it is the object of their descendants scorn! It even made one of Europe's most noted writers and historians of the 18th Century C.E. cried out in anger when he witnessed his fellow Europeans treatment of the descendants of the Nile Valley High-Cultures of biblical times, Egypt and Nubia particularly:

> There a people now forgotten discovered while others were yet barbarians, the elements of the arts and sciences. A race of men now rejected for their black skin, and woolly hair, founded on the study of the laws of nature those civil and religious systems which still govern the universe.

Count C.F. Volney's outcry is sufficient to conclude this PRELUDE to the following text. And of course, it too assisted me to present the necessary documentation normally required to prove to certain people "academic veracity." This is expected of me, even if I had taken my facts from European and European-American "scholars" and "academicians" whose evidence of the same may have been total distortions or outright lies in the first place. But, I wish to assure you that I only used original sources whenever I drew conclusions. And, of course, I made certain that extra precaution was taken in checking secondary sources..., etc. Yet in this Volume, as in all of the other volumes I have written to date, I have not used Europeans and European-Americans in any field of discipline as the sole "AUTHORITY ON AFRICA, AFRICANS" and/or "THINGS AFRICAN:" references

---

1. The WHITE NILE begins in Uganda, at Mwanza Nyanza; the BLUE NILE in Ethiopia, at Lake Take Tana.
2. The ATBARA RIVER begins in the Highlands of Ethiopia, north of Lake Tana.
3. Mwanza Nyanza, Tanganyika Nyanza and Malawi Nyanza. "NYANZA" means "LAKE."
4. See C.F. Volney's RUINS OF EMPIRE, London, 1800-?, p. 17; originally published

to them being solely for academic requirements in this institution. Materials extracted from European and European-American "educators," and other types of "writers'" works, are only for citation and criticism as they affect African peoples throughout the entire world; for I am most certain that the only "AUTHORITATIVE SOURCES ON AFRICA, AFRICAN PEOPLE" and/or "THINGS AFRICAN" are first vested in African [BLACK] People; and all others after. Thus it is; the best historian is the person who was personally involved in the facts of the story being told, as each person's account of the same story is influenced and prejudiced by his [or her] personal interest to the facts. In this very light, we can see that a slave and his master cannot have the same interest in the slave's overall welfare; because the master sees his slave as property to insure and increase his own wealth. The slave, on the other hand, sees his master as the evil genius of cultural and physical genocide. These facts equally hold true for the descendants of the slave and master from the same set of historical events and facts of the history of the entire WORLD as we knew it yesterday, and know it today.

In view of all I have said so far; is it not a fact that the slave's understanding of his role in GENESIS will vary dramatically to that of his [or her] master's version? Thus it is that in GENESIS the Africans who worshipped Ywh before the so-called "FIVE BOOKS OF MOSES, OLD TESTAMENT" or "HOLY TORAH" had to present a different basis of acceptance for their own "CHOSEN PEOPLE'S"..."ONE AND ONLY TRUE GOD" and "PROMISE LAND" myth that was different to the Africans who worshipped Ra; those of the God YWH carefully forgetting the fact that the source of their religious belief is still in the teachings of the Nile Valley Africans MYSTERIES SYSTEM of the Grand Lodge of Luxor - which taught that:

"IN THE BEGINNING WAS THE WORD."

Whose "WORD?" This biblical concept was uttered by the Africans who worshipped the Sun God - RA, AMEN-RA, PTAH-RA, etc. for thousands upon thousands of years before there was a Hebrew God named YWH [Jehovah]. Said teaching is still present in the BOOK OF THE COMING FORTH BY DAY AND BY NIGHT [Egyptian Book Of The Dead and Papyrus Of Ani]. Such an irrefutable fact finds no place or comfort among those who still prefer to make their parishoners believe that the entire WORLD of mankind began with the Mosaic drama that was enacted by the following characters or superstars:

> "YWH, ADAM, EVE, NOAH, ABRAHAM, JACOB, ISAAC, JOSEPH, ISAIAH, MOSES, DAVID, SOLOMON, JESUS CHRIST, MOHAMET ibn ABDULLAH...,"

---

in French about 1792 C.E. at Paris, France. Volney was with Napoleon Boneparte when he invaded Egypt, with the intent of capturing it for fellow French imperialists.

et al. But they too know very well that mankind, and religion, existed for thousands upon thousands of years before the Hebrew, Christian and Moslem superstars' GENESIS. This is providing we have not forgotten our so-called "PAGAN PAST" - viz-a-viz our own SUN worship, FIRE worship, ANIMAL worship, HUMAN worship and SEX worship's GENESIS.

LECTURE No. I

BLACK PHILOSOPHY: THE GENESIS OF JUDAISM, CHRISTIANITY, ISLAM AND "WESTERN CIVILIZATION."

When a white student in my BLACK PHILOSOPHY class at Rutgers University, Newark Campus, Newark, New Jersey questioned...

> "the validity of the presumption that Africans were in fact related to the development of a body of philosophical conclusions before the Europeans of Greece... ,"

it was not at all astonishing to me that most of my black students equally shared the same concern. This, of course, even though they were, for the most part, only suggesting the question by the shifting of their eyes, along with the grimaces on their countenance. But the real challenge began when I pointed out that:

> "Aristotle attempted to prove that his fellow Greek named Thales, who allegedly lived between ca. 620 and 545 B.C.E., was the first person on record that developed the following concepts in his teaching.... That:
> [a] Water is the source of all living things; and
> [b] All things are full of God."[1]

Without refering to the indigenous African concepts from whence the Greeks received their information for [a] and [b], we know they were taken from among the Nile Valley MYSTERIES SYSTEM'S texts. Thus, I had only to bring to the attention of all of the students that an African named "MOSES," a son of Egypt,[2] had already passed this down from his fellow African teachers[3] sometime following ca. 1232 B.C.E., which, of course, was at least 612 years before the birth of Thales - the first of the so-called "PRE-SOCRATIC GREEK PHILOSOPHERS;" if in fact they ever lived?

Certainly the ancestors of Moses did not pass down to him any of the conclusions which they had developed in the Asian desert. Their own records show that they did not develop any written document until hundreds of years following the mysterious burial of Moses on

1. Turner's HISTORY OF PHILOSOPHY , p. 34.
2. The Hebrew HOLY TORAH [Old Testament] states that Moses was born in the City of Succoth, Egypt, which is in Northeast Africa. See EXODUS ii : 1 - 10
3. They ancestors established the Grand Lodge of Luxor and its Subordinate Lodges in Asia and Europe. [See BLACK MAN OF THE NILE AND HIS FAMILY, p. 252].

Mount Sinai - a mountain in Egypt, Northeast Africa.[1]

The so-called "TEACHINGS OF MOSES" in GENESIS, his "FIRST BOOK," particularly with reference to "THE CREATION OF MAN OUT OF THE CLAY OF THE EARTH," or whatever else, which Abraham's[2] God - YWH [Jehovah or Adoni, Adonoi] - supposedly did, was not done without "WATER" - the source of every living things. But the "SOURCE" of all living things for the Africans along the Northeastern section of Africa was already "WATER," represented by the God called "HAPI" - otherwise "THE GOD OF THE RIVER NILE."[3]

The River Nile [both BLUE and WHITE affluents] was dominant in the socio-political, socio-economic, and philosophical mythology and religious life-style of each and every ancient indigenous African of each and every Nile Valley High-Culture. With regards to Egypt, it was "THE SOURCE OF LIFE ITSELF - GOD."

If the River Nile was to the ancient Africans who lived along its banks "The Source Of All Life...," it stands to reason that it was in fact to said Africans...

"THE BEGINNING [Genesis] OF ALL THINGS" -

God or Hapi. Yet we find the theory of man's origin, as stated in the BOOK OF THE COMING FORTH BY DAY AND BY NIGHT,[4] was at least before the Ist Dynasty [ca. 4100 B.C.E.], which preceded the arrival of the first non-indigenous invaders of Egypt... the "HYKSOS" or "SHEPHERD KINGS OF BEDUINA;" all of this when Egypt was still called "TA-MERRY, KIMIT, KAMT, PEARL OF THE NILE," etc., and the people - ROMITI. Of course this was more than 2825 years before Moses developed his allegorical story about..."NOAH AND THE GREAT DELUGE" [flood], along with his naming of parts of Africa - "EGYPT, KUSH" and "PUNT" - in honour of Noah's grandsons of like names; all of this according to GENESIS, Chapter x, Verses 1 - 32. In the same context we find the following in GENESIS, Chapter i, Verses 1 - 9:

> 1 [The Story of Creation] In the beginning God created the heavens and the earth;[2] the earth was waste and void; darkness covered the abyss, and the spirit of God was stirring above the waters.
> 3 God said, "Let there be light," and there was light. God saw that the light was good.[4] God separated the light from the darkness, calling the light Day and the darkness Night.[5] And there was evening and morning, the first day.

---

1. DEUTERONOMY xxxiv : 1 - 6. See p. 54 of this Lecture for location of Mount Sinai.
2. The first member of the Haribu [Hebrew, Israelite or Jewish] religion.
3. DEUTERONOMY xxxiv : 1 - 6.
4. See E.A.W. Budge, EGYPTIAN BOOK OF THE DEAD and PAPYRUS OF ANI, p. 174.

On the other hand, we also find the following in the BOOK OF THE COMING FORTH BY DAY AND BY NIGHT [English translation by Sir E.A.W. Budge, Egyptian Book of the Dead, p. 174]:

> [Khnemu was] -the father in the beginning," 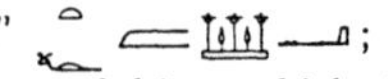; "the Maker of "things which are. Creator of things which shall be. Source "of the lands, Father of fathers, Mother of mothers,"
> 
> "Father of the fathers of the gods and goddesses, lord of "things created in himself, maker of heaven, and earth, and "the Ṭuat, and water, and the mountains," 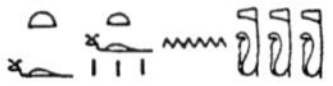
> ; "supporter of the sky upon its four pillars, raised up of the same in the firmament (?)"
> 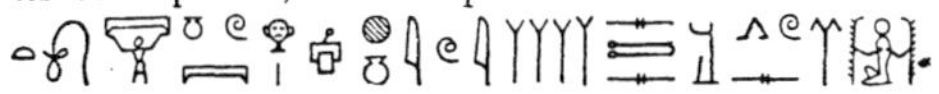

With respect to the former I have not questioned the veracity of the facts stated, neither of the existence of a person named Thales who, supposedly, lived in Greece around ca. 620 - 546 B.C.E.; nor of the person named MOSES, who was born in the City of Succoth, Egypt [Northeast Africa] during the XIXth Dynasty at a period when Pharaoh Haremheb's [ca. 1340 - 1320 B.C.E.] son Pharaoh Rameses I [ca. 1320 - 1318 B.C.E.] reigned over Egypt. But, there is no argument presented here as to the fact or fiction of the last two men's existence. The main issue of contention is whether or not Thales, Moses, or someone else, was in fact the first to project the two concepts of the philosophical conclusions I have introduced as items [a] and [b] before. As for the Hebrew's, or Israelite's, chronology dealing with Moses' religious origin, he told his own story. Thales, on the other hand, forced us to depend heavily upon the chronological evidence presented by a Greek stoic named Eratosthenes, who lived around ca. 274 - 194 B.C.E. Eratosthenes was later supported by other Greeks - Apollodorus about ca. 140 B.C.E., Adronicus ca. 70 - 60 B.C.E., and last Diogenes Laertius. Yet, it was not until Aristotle sacked the Library of the Grand Lodge of Luxor [Thebes] in ca. 327 B.C.E., and brought into Egypt hundreds of Greek students to study under African priests who taught them the ancient philosophical concepts and secrets of the Nile Valley

Africans MYSTERIES SYSTEM,[1] that the Greeks compiled most of the other works so-called "modern" academicians call "GREEK PHILOSOPHY."

One can continue, almost endlessly, pointing out the inconsistencies of the claims European and European-American educators have made for their Greek forefathers who, allegedly, brought them into "CIVILIZATION" by way of their own education they received from the ancient Africans and Asians; the same facts hold true for the Hebrews past, and present. Nevertheless, it is first with the willful attempt to perpetually distort the dramas in the so-called FIVE BOOKS OF MOSES [Holy Torah or Old Testament], particularly GENESIS and EXODUS [the First and Second of the Five Books], I must deal with in respect to their "modern" [European and European-American] distortions, much of which we can best observe in the teachings of the LATTER DAY SAINTS [Mormons] of the United States of America and the JOHN CALVIN type of racists and religious bigots who delegated unto themselves the job of protectors of God - in this case JESUS CHRIST. This, of course, is no exception to certain leaders of Judaism who carefully allowed the myth of a "JEWISH [Semitic] RACE," which color is "WHITE," to go unchallenged among the worshippers of both YWH and JESUS CHRIST.

Examining the theory of the role of "THE CREATOR OF THE WORLD" myth thousands of years before Moses came forward with his own version in the BOOK OF GENESIS, as attributed to him by Hebrew rabbis hundreds of years following his death and burial, we find other indigenous Africans of the Nile Valley High-Cultures writing sometime around ca. 4100 B.C.E. in what is today called the "PAPYRUS OF NESI-ANSU,"[2] that:

> "...only the great God NEB-ER-TCHER existed before the creation of the world and all that followed in it thereafter, as even the Gods were not yet born."

In the BOOK OF THE COMING FORTH BY DAY AND BY NIGHT we find the great God NEB-ER-TCHER saying the following:

> "I brought my mouth, and I uttered my own name as a word of power, and thus I evolved myself under my own name as a word of power, and thus I evolve myself under the evolutions of the God Khepera, and I developed myself out of the premival matter which had evolved multitudes of evolutions from the beginning of time. Nothing existed on earth, I made all things. There was none other who worked with me at that time."

Let us also examine the same origin as taught by the African we call "Moses," the man

---

1. William Turner's HISTORY OF PHILOSOPHY, pp. 158 - 159 reminds us that Aristotle made certain that his two prize students, Theophrastus and Eudemus, continued plagiarizing the philosophical teachings of the Nile Valley Africans, even following his own death.
2. See Sir E.A. Wallis Budge's writings in ARCHAEOLOGIA, vol. LII, London, 1891.

charged with being responsible for handing down to the Hebrews, Christians and Moslems the basic...

> "TEACHINGS ABOUT CREATION" [he] "RECEIVED FROM YWH[1] ON MOUNT SINAI...," etc. [in Northeast Egypt, Northeast Africa].

Thus in GENESIS we find Moses telling the same story in the following manner to his fellow illiterate Hebrews that were not able, unlike Moses, to attend the MYSTERIES at the Grand Lodge of Luxor:

> 1 [Story of Creation] In the beginning God created........ [etc. See page
> 6 of this Lecture for Verses 1 through 5].
> 6 Then God said, "let there be a firmament in the midst of the waters to
> divide the waters." And so it was. 7 God made the firmament, dividing the
> waters that were below the firmament from those that were above it. God
> called the firmament Heaven. And there was evening and morning, the
> second day.
> 9 Then God said. "Let the waters below the heavens be gathered into one
> place and let the dry land appear." And so it was. 10 God called the dry
> land Earth and the assembled waters Seas. And God saw that it was good.
> 11 Then God said." Let the earth bring forth vegetation: seed-bearing
> plants and all kinds of fruit trees that bear fruit containing seed.[1]

What we have seen in the GENESIS of both of these Africans is that the "WORD" alone is GOD. And that from the mere utterance of the "WORD" said "GOD" made everything - "MAN, ANIMALS" and "THINGS." In the "WORD" is the "POWER" to it all.

One has to be totally irresponsible and fanatically bias not to recognize Moses attempt at detailing the teachings he learnt as an "INITIATE" in the Mysteries System at the Grand Lodge of Luxor [Thebes]. For it would have been impossible for Moses, or anyone else in Egypt at that period, to have raised to one of the highest rank in the government of Pharaoh Rameses IInd's "Inner Circle" [Cabinet or Chamber] and was not himself trained in the religious rites of the Mysteries under the priests of the religion of God - AMEN-RA. Moses himself was raised to the ranks of "HIEROGRAMMAT" and "PRIEST." Like Jesus Christ..., he too received his final "INITIATION" into the Mysteries at the Great Pyramid Of Khufu.[2]

Analyzing the entire posibility of Moses being able to divest himself of everything he learnt in school from his fellow African teachers and priests; could it have been possible for him to remember WORD FOR WORD everything Ywh allegedly revealed to him on Mount Sinai without the benefit of a notebook, stenographer or tape recorder? Certainly the

---

1. This name was originally used in Egypt before the birth of the first Hebrew - Abraham. He was popular during the XXVIth Dynasty as a minor divine figure under the name of YWH, YAHWA, YAWHE, etc., and written in Hieroglyph 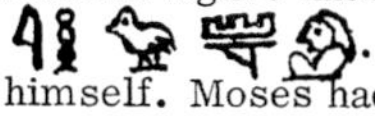. The first four [4] letters mean DIVINITY; the last is a picture of YWH himself. Moses had to read about him long before this period. See BLACK MAN OF THE NILE AND HIS FAMILY, p. 344.
2. Herodotus referred to Pharaoh Khufu as "CHEOPS" or "KHEOPS;" other ancient Greeks

"TABLET OF LAWS" which "YWH GAVE MOSES ON MOUNT SINAI" was not a compilation of manuscripts or written documents. Also, there is no document on record written in Moses' handwriting we can check for the stories attributed to him. In this case, as with that of Jesus Christ of Nazareth, we are relying solely upon third to fifth-hand sources for our only basis of "TRUTH" with respect to "GOD'S [Ywh] REVELATIONS." In both of these stories the recipients were already dead for hundreds of years before anyone wrote down what they allegedly told other parties - all of whom were equally dead before the HOLY TORAH [Five Books Of Moses or Old Testament] was written by certain Hebrew writers, and translated into Greek while the Hebrews were already subjected to GREEK MYTHOLOGY in Greece.

If we examine the geographic location of the entire "WORLD OF GENESIS" we will find a map like that following on page 64 of this Volume. Yet this was not the "WORLD" Moses and Abraham knew. They knew completely different "WORLDS." On page 35 we see Moses and Abraham's "WORLDS." Abraham's "WORLD" was around ca. 1675 B.C.E.; Moses' "WORLD" came much later in ca. 1300 - 1232 B.C.E. During these periods the indigenous Africans of the Nile Valley's "INSPIRED WORKS OF GOD...[Râ]" had already passed through at least one edit from an original dated before ca. 4100 B.C.E., which was shortly before the founding of the Ist Dynasty by Pharaoh Aha[1] from Nubia.

Therefore, when one speaks about...

"THE GENEALOGY OF THE PEOPLE OF THE NEW WORLD...,"

according to GENESIS, Chapter v, Verses 1 - 32, and Chapter ix, Verses 1 - 9, or even Chapter ii through xxxvi, one must presuppose that no other people existed in the "WORLD" but those descended from "ADAM" and "EVE" before the "GREAT DELUGE" [or Flood], and from "NOAH" and his wife following the "GREAT DELUGE;" all of which was written by Hebrew scribes for a Hebrew nation and religion. In this case one has to discount the fact that many ancient Africans wrote their own stories about...

"THE BEGINNING OF THE WORLD" [and its inhabitants] "GENEAOLOGY"

thousands of years before the birth of the first Hebrew - AVRAM or ABRAHAM, and many hundreds more before the birth of the first of the educated Hebrews - MOSHE or MOSES. Of

---

and Romans called him "CECROPS." See Brucker's CRITICAL HISTORY OF PHILOSOPHY; H.S. Lewis' MYSTICAL LIFE OF JESUS; C.H. Vail's ANCIENT MYSTERIES; A. Besant's ESOTERIC CHRISTIANITY; M. Müller's MYTHOLOGY OF EGYPT; G.G.M. James' STOLEN LEGACY.

1. Pharaoh AHA was called "MENES" by Herodotus. He was also known as "NARMER" among

course it is difficult to understand why any God - YWH, JESUS CHRIST or AL'LAH - would have allowed the predecessors of Noah, Abraham and Moses to preach for thousands of years before his own "INSPIRED WORDS" were handed down to Moses. But, was it false information the others before Noah, Abraham and **Moses** preached? Was God not aware of what was taking place without any of his "COMMANDMENTS" being used by the people he had created? One would assume that God's people were allowed to live without any body of laws - "COMMANDMENTS" - from the first day of the "CREATION OF THE WORLD" to about ca. 1192 B.C.E. For, chronologically speaking, it was about that period of time that:

"MOSES RECEIVED THE TEN COMMANDMENTS ON MOUNT SINAI"...

and passed them down to...

"GOD'S CHOSEN PEOPLE"...

[Hebrews, Israelites or Jews]. This, of course, is outside of the "LAW" against eating of "EVIL" products "GOD" made before there was even a "DEVIL" - the so-called...

"FORBIDDEN FRUIT TREE"...,

which God himself placed in the "GARDEN OF EDEN" to trap both "ADAM and EVE."

Now, let us deal with another basic "TRUTH" of the further suppression of religious facts; such as Moses did not write a single "WORD" of what we call the BOOK OF GENESIS, or BOOK OF THE BEGINNINGS. As a matter of fact, the final edition of Chapters i through xi of GENESIS was **not written** until the Fifth [5th] Century B.C.E. by one or more unknown Hebrew authors. Moses was already dead for approximately five hundred [500] years, from about the Tenth [10th] Century B.C.E. And in those writers prehistoric recordings of things that allegedly happened thousands upon thousands of years prior to Abraham's birth, muchless their own, all amounted to nothing more than Hebrew FOLK-LORE. From GENESIS, Chapter i through xi the entire FIVE BOOKS OF MOSES rest solely upon six [6] main alleged TRUTHS; and everyone of them were equally mentioned in the mythology of the BOOK OF THE COMING FORTH BY DAY AND BY NIGHT[1] by the indigenous African scribes of the Nile Valley Mysteries System of the Grand Lodge of Luxor, and before. They are:

First: An unknown identity - "GOD" - created itself out of nothing; then proceeded to make every aspect of everything we see and cannot see, solely upon its commands by the "WORD;"

---

his fellow Africans along the Nile Valley. His original home was around the Second Cataract in Nubia [Ta-Nehisi or Zeti; part of today's Sudan].

1. It is also known as the EGYPTIAN BOOK OF THE DEAD and PAPYRUS OF ANI.

Second: The same God made an image of himself and placed into it a "SOUL" - thus the first "MAN" [Adam], the original human from whom...the first "WOMAN" [Eve] and all other people of the Judaeo-Christian-Islamic "world;"

Third: The establishment of everything, including the "first man" and "woman," was made inferior to God - thus their sinful offsprings [mankind like ourselves];

Fourth: The state of total obedience was made the everlasting reward for happiness through morality, which God demanded of the "first man" and his mate's descendants as their payment for "immortality" or "everlasting divinity;"

Fifth: Man and woman's inferiority was dramatized by their fall from God's Holy Grace - thus their eternal condemnation due to their knowledge of sexual intercourse, equally the denial of "man" and "woman" being the sole producers of human beings - Gods like the original "CREATOR;"

Sixth: The reward and penalty syndrome. God established "GOOD" and "EVIL." He then created the "DEVIL" with apparently more power than himself, permitting said "EVIL" to capture the imagination of His most precious creation - Human beings, all of whom "...He gave dominion over all other living things...," etc., etc., etc., almost endlessly.

The previous "TRUTHS" are compelling upon everyone living in any society where Judaism, Christianity or Islam is the dominant religion in the control of those who rule. Here in the United States of America it is basically Christianity, with a very heavy infusion of WHITE RACIAL PURITY and an overdose of JUDAEO-SEMITISM, that control our every move. Of course all of this is denied; and like the writer, or writers, of GENESIS, Chapter i, Verse 11, those who rule and control most of us through the alleged teachings of our Gods [Jehovah or Jesus Christ] act as if in fact within this country, the United States of America, there is truly a...

"SEPARATION BETWEEN RELIGION [church] AND GOVERNMENT [state],"

and point to the Federal Constitution[1] for their documentation, forgetting, however, that the "WORDS" therein are equally translated into action as distortedly as those in GENESIS.

Since man and woman must certainly die, and their body normally rot before, and after, they enter the earth, it is only natural that the Africans and Asians of the ancient "WORLD" would have developed and earth-like man and woman that were kneaded into existence by the "Great [one and only] God." Thus we find that the same theory was independently developed among the MALEKULA people of the New Hebrides. Their God - BOKOR - also kneaded

---

1. See Amendment I, UNITED STATES CONSTITUTION:"Congress shall make no law for the establishment of religion...," etc.

their own world's...

"FIRST MAN AND WOMAN OUT OF CLAY"...,

etc. according to F.L.U. Laggat's "Maleluka, New Hebrides" [in: Report of the Fourth Meeting of the Australasian Association for the Advancement of Science, Hobart 1893, 707f]. But among the Africans of Egypt the potter God - KHNUM - was the one who moulded man on his pottery wheel; thus we see him doing the same in the bas-reliefs at the Temple of Luxor, where the birth of Queen Hatshep-sut,and Pharaoh Amenhotep III,are depicted. During the so-called "First Intermediary Period Of The Egyptian Empire [ca. 2300 - 2050 B.C.E.]" it was also shown that:

"KHNUM" [God] " CAN NO LONGER FASHION MORTALS."

In the "Instruction Of Amen-em-opet," which was written sometime around the Seventh [VIIth] Century B.C.E. however, we find the following about the composition of man:

"BUT MAN WAS MADE FROM CLAY AND STRAW,
WITH GOD AS HIS BUILDER."

There are countless other stories of "CREATION" all around the "WORLD" of yesterday and today. Each cultural [tribal] grouping in Africa, Asia, Europe and the Americas, etc. has its own "ONLY TRUE CREATION" story. And, each has its proof to show that its "PROPHET" or "PROPHETS" told the people of the entire "WORLD" about the "ONLY TRUE WORDS INSPIRED BY GOD." Yet each man or woman in each group, who is rooted into his or her particular cultural and religious ethnocentricity, believes HE or SHE belongs to the purest...

"CHOSEN PEOPLE OF THE ONE AND ONLY TRUE GOD."

Of course...GOD...could not have selected any other "INSPIRED SCRIBES" than from his own "CHOSEN PEOPLE" - those telling the story. Here is the GENESIS of religious bigotry and racial prejudice. Certainly this kind of observation and analysis is dangerous to most of the members of the clergy, particularly those who are afraid that their followers may question the validity of their Saturday or Sunday mythologies and allegories they are presenting as...

"THE ONLY GOD-GIVEN INSPIRED WORDS"...

in the form of the actual historical dramas and stories; all of which they protect with:

"IN THE BEGINNING THERE WAS THE WORD, AND THE WORD WAS GOD."

Whose "WORD" was there? Was it that of the God RA - the Sun, the oldest of the Gods of man who was always here, so far as we can tell? Was it the God YWH [Jehovah] of the Hebrews, who did not make his appearance in the "WORLD" until ca. 1675 - 1640 B.C.E.

in the dreams of Abraham, and still later in the teachings of Moses and his alleged "FIVE BOOKS?" Was it the God JESUS CHRIST of Nazareth, who followed 1675 or 1640 years of Jewish history before he was born of a Jewish mother - "MARY" - without the benefit of a father of any kind as other men [except "Adam"] better than 1973 years ago? Or was it the God AL'LAH, who came out of the City of Mecca and Medina in the Arabian Peninsula no more than 622 years following the death of the Christians' God - JESUS CHRIST, which in itself was no more than 1352 years ago? Why could it not have been the God OLEDUMARE of the Yorubas of Nigeria, ~~West Africa~~; the God NGAI of the Agikuyu of Kenya, East Africa; the God DAMBALLAH OUEDO of the African-Caribbean people of Haiti; or the God THUNDERBIRD of the so-called "Indians" and "Caribs" of the Caribbean Sea and the Americas? Because the writers, allegedly "...GOD'S INSPIRED SCRIBES...," etc. in each of their own GENESIS, envision their very tiny [almost fantastically minute] "WORLD" as the only important one, which their "ONE AND ONLY TRUE GOD HAS CHOSEN" for them to dominate [enslave]. This concept the "GOD INSPIRED SCRIBES" even perpetuate to the point where all of mankind must accept; and if not, coerced to endorse as... "THE ONE AND ONLY TRUE BASIS OF RELIGION." The epitome of this type of arrogance was best expressed by the Moslem "JIHADS" [Holy Wars], six CHRISTIAN CRUSADES, and the Jewish "CHOSEN PEOPLE" religious bigotry and racism imbeded in their alleged "SEMITIC PURITY" which supposedly justified their extermination of the Canaanites and the seizure of their land.

The Messianic syndrome even perverted African [BLACK] People, to the extent that they too became like the self-appointed masters against all who were, and are, different to themselves. This was accomplished through their own brainwashing by the perpetuators of Talmudic Judaism, Roman and Protestant Christianity, and every form of Islam. But it equally made BLACKS [African peoples] hate themselves and their "AFRICAN HERITAGE" that became "THE ROOT OF WESTERN CIVILIZATION" passed down to the Europeans - Greeks, etc.

GENESIS of the Jewish, Christian and Islamic religions is no different, in terms of the importance of "WATER" preceding everything else, than GENESIS of the Gabons of the Republic of Zaire[1] or the Yorubas of the Republic of Nigeria.[2] And the "WIND" from God's mouth that allegedly separated creation's "WATERS" into the primordial "DEEP" and primordial "FIRMAMENT" [heaven] is also shown separating the "WATERS OF THE REED SEA"[not Red Sea] of Egypt for the African Jews of Egypt.[3] But another "WIND" had already

1. R.P. Trilles, "Les pygmees de la foret equatoriale," Paris, 1933, p. 72.
2. L. Frobenius, "Die altlantische Gotterlechre," Atlantis 10 [1926], p. 109.
3. See EXODUS xv : 8 - 10.

blown from the "MOUTH OF AMUN", who was the God of the Africans of Egypt Moses had to worship before he was able to write his own religious teachings for the Hebrews,[1] much of which he took from the Egyptian "STORY OF CREATION" in THE BOOK OF KNOWING HOW RA CAME INTO BEING - which is written in Hieroglyph:

and as told by the God NEBERTCHER  ....the "Everlasting God of the Universe."[2]

GENESIS is by no means believable [as we can see in the previous quotation] any more so than the other four BOOKS OF MOSES [Old Testament or Holy Torah]. For in GENESIS we find that the Hebrew God - YWH - made "MAN" before he made the "BEASTS," and equally the "BEASTS" before "MAN." Thus GENESIS, Chapter i, Verses 25 - 26 states:

> And God made the beasts of the earth after his kind, and cattle after their kind, and everything that creepeth upon the earth after his kind; and God saw that it was good. And God said, "Let us make man in our image, after our likeness."

Here we see that God [the Jewish and Christian god-head] made the "BEASTS" before he made man. But GENESIS, Chapter ii, Verses 18 - 20 recites the following:

> And the Lord God said, "It is not good that the man should be alone; I will make him an help meet for him." And out of the ground the Lord God formed every beast of the field, and every fowl of the air; and brought them unto Adam....but for Adam there was not an help meet for him.

The "inspired writers of God," or was it God himself, seemed not to have kept proper chronological records of which came first, "MAN" or "BEASTS." But these contradictions are only two of the hundreds that appear throughout the so-called "FIVE BOOKS OF MOSES." Thus in GENESIS, Chapter ii, Verse 17 we find God [YWH] laying down his "FIRST COMMANDMENT " with respect to Adam's longivity - saying:

> "But of the tree of the knowledge of good and evil thou shalt not eat of it: for in the day thou eatest thereof thou shalt surely die."

Yet, Adam ate of the forbidden "TREE" and did not "SURELY DIE"..."IN THE DAY" [he ate][3] "THEREOF;" as it was not until hundreds of years later before he died. For we also read in GENESIS, Chapter v, Verse 5 the following:

> And all the days that Adam lived were nine hundred and thirty years; and he died.

---

1. See EXODUS xv : 8 - 10
2. See EGYPTIAN HIERATIC PAPYRI IN THE BRITISH MUSEUM, London, 1910.
3. See K. Sethe's AMUN, 1909, p. 97.

Since GENESIS ends where EXODUS begins, it is equally important that I end this phase of my biblical citations with the following from EXODUS, Chapter xii, Verse 40:

> Now the sojourning of the children of Israel, who dwelt in Egypt, was four hundred and thirty years.

On the other hand ACTS, Chapter vii, Verse 6 contradicts the chronological reporting in EXODUS, Chapter xii, Verse 40 which I read before. It states:

> And God spake on this wise, that his seed should sojourn in a strange land; and that they should bring them into bondage, and entreat them evil four hundred years.

Anyone can see that there is thirty [30] years difference between 430 and 400 years. However Jacob and his sons entered Egypt, Northeast Africa just about 214 to 215 years following the so-called "CALL" [in his dream] "OF ABRAHAM" by Ywh; and approximately 112 years following Abraham's death. If the HOLY BIBLE is correct, and this we must believe if it is "...the inspired WORDS of God..." according to the teachings of the Jewish, Christian and Moslem clergy, then the descendants of Jacob and his sons could not have slaved in Egypt for more than 215 or 216 years maximum duration.

I hope that we have been looking at our biblical map and taking very careful notation of the geography involved in the drama I have just mentioned, and all before that in GENESIS and EXODUS. It covers the continuous stretch of landmass in both Africa and Asia we now call the "MIDDLE EAST" geo-politically. We must equally remember that in this area of land only African and Asian peoples lived the periods of the dramas in question. At least, no other people than those of "Canaan" [Genesis, Chapter xvii, Verse 8] and "Egypt" [Genesis, Chapter xlvi, Verses 26 - 27] are mentioned so far in these dramas. Thus when we re-examine the geographic location, and the peoples concerned, we find that during those periods most of the ancient Europeans [Greeks, Etruscans and Romans] were not even in existence no where in the history of the known "WORLD" of GENESIS or EXODUS; thus no "WESTERN"[European-White-Caucasian]"CIVILIZATION."

Examining even closer than we have done so far, we discover that it was the land of the "CURSED" descendants of Ham - the "CANAANITES," otherwise the so-called "NEGROES," that Jehovah allegedly selected to give his "CHOSEN PEOPLE" - the Hebrews - to make their PROMISEDLAND. This was the same land that certain Sixth Century C.E. European rabbis and Talmudists wrote about in the following distorted manner in their own ethnic and racist version of GENESIS, Chapter ix, Verses 25 - 27 of the BABYLONIAN TALMUD.... Noah, speaking to his sons, supposedly said:

Now I cannot beget the fourth son whose children I would have ordered to serve you and your brothers! Therefore it must be Canaan, your first born, whom they enslave. And since you have disabled me...doing ugly things in blackness of night, Canaan's children shall be born ugly and black! Moreover, because you twisted your head around to see my nakedness, your grandchildren's hair shall be twisted into kinks; and their eyes red; again because your lips jested at my misfortune, theirs shall swell; and because you neglected my nakedness, they shall go naked, and their male members shall be shamefully elongated! Men of this race are called Negroes, their forefather Canaan commanded them to love theft and fornication, to be banded together in hatred of their masters and never to tell the truth. 1

First: I suppose we are to overlook the fact that Noah was allowed to act as God in cursing people; and that Ywh gave "CURSED" land to His own "CHOSEN PEOPLE." Those writers seemed to have been too racist to observe what their God - YWH - was doing to their own ancestors [White or Semitic-Caucasian] who, supposedly, were not "CURSED."

Second: If "CANAAN" became the "PROMISELAND," it would mean that present day Israel stands upon the land that was formerly owned by "CURSED...NEGROES" [black people] like those of the Sixth Century C.E. Babylonian Talmud's GENESIS, Chap. ix, 25 - 27. Obviously, they were the same "NEGROES" as the people of the "HARLEMS" of the United States of America who were, and still are, descendants of "NOAH," his son "HAM," and his grandson "CANAAN," according to the biblical story we have just read.

The next issue we have to consider is the so-called "GENEALOGY OF THE SEMITES" [Shemites] according to GENESIS, Chapter ix, Verses 20 - 28, which was the same as that of the Hamites [Chamites]. For "SHEM, HAM" and "JAPHETH" were "THE SONS OF NOAH" [or Noe], which he produced with the same mother. Thus, even if the alleged "CURSE" was other than the allegorical racist myth it is, these three - Shem, Ham and Japheth - remained full brothers. At least the "SEMITES" - descendants of Shem- would be still COUSINS of the "HAMITES" - descendants of Ham...whose children were the "CANAANITES" - the so-called "NEGROES." It must be noted that not a single "CAUCASIAN," so far, is mentioned

1. See Robert Graves and Robert Patai, HEBREW MYTHS, p. 121; also a similar article in the OLD TESTAMENT OF THE HOLY BIBLE [Confraternity Version, Guild Press, New York, 1961], footnote comments by Rev. Joseph Grispino, S.M.L. commenting on the alleged racial references by Noah; and Y. ben-Jochannan, AFRICA: MOTHER OF "WESTERN CIVILIZATION. Words underscored in order to emphasize where much of the unnatural fear of the BLACK MAN sexuality syndrome originated. Because of the gravity and implication this story presents I have carefully check out the supportive documentation in Hebrew Myths and found them to be totally reliable. Further elaboration on the above aspect of this continued racism by more modern Jews see Y. ben-Jochannan's CULTURAL GENOCIDE IN THE BLACK AND AFRICAN STUDIES CURRICULUM; J.A. Rogers' WORLD'S GREAT MEN OF COLOR.

in any of these African-Asian dramas, even as racist as the "INSPIRED SCRIBES" were in the "WORLD OF THE BIBLE;" as during this period [Genesis and Exodus] no Hebrew scribe knew of a "CAUCASUS MOUNTAIN" or its "CAUCASIAN PEOPLE."

It is noteworthy that Ywh, who condemned drunkeness, would have accepted and condoned Noah's drunken stupor - to the point where he rediculously exposed his genital organs and other parts of his anatomy. Ywh did not punish Noe, but instead punished Noah's youngest son - Ham who knew no better than to joke about his father's making a disgraceful spectacle of himself in public. Surely the wrongdoer was Noah! If anyone, logically that is, should have been "CURSED;" why not Noah...the drunkard?

There could be no doubt that the early Hebrews were caught in a period of "SEXUAL HANG-UPS" during the GENESIS of their very young nation. Also, that they were reacting against the "FERTILITY RIGHTS" they once practiced in the Nile Valley, particularly in Egypt. For the extreme penalty placed upon entire "races" and "generations" of people by Ywh, because of a SEX disoriented drama, even reverted to the first two people - "ADAM" and "EVE" - Ywh made perfect, only to have them commit "THE FIRST SIN" - sexual intercourse. We cannot overlook the fact that the Hebrew writers who wrote this folk-lore could have been influenced by the prevailing SEXUAL syndrome of their era...the Greek myth about the castration of one of their Gods named CROMUS by his three sons - Posudon, Zeus and Hades. Like Ham, Zeus was also "...the youngest son..." of Cromus. However, unlike Ham's misfortune, Zeus became the "GOD [king] OF HEAVEN" after his father's castration. And at least, Cromus was punished for his wrongdoing; not his son - Zeus.

The Hebrew writer, or writers, of GENESIS even hid behind a treacherous and diabolical God-Mother figure in the person of "EVE." Instead of the MOTHER OF YWH [their God], like many other religions of their ancient origin and area, she became the MOTHER OF THE "ORIGINAL SIN" [sexual intercourse], a role she assumed before there was even a "DEVIL." As such, she took away ADAM'S motherhood ; and as a direct result of her "ORIGINAL SIN" people began reproducing themselves through her "ORIGINAL VAGINA" instead of Abraham's Ywh's "ORIGINAL CLAY" or Adam's "ORIGINAL RIB."

The last point in this Lecture I will raise is; to whom Ywh was speaking when he allegedly said:

"LET US MAKE MAN IN OUR OWN IMAGE, AFTER OUR OWN LIKENESS?"

---

1. It must be noted that the Roman Catholic version of the woman, MARY, was that she remained a "PHYSICAL VIRGIN" even after she had James "the lesser" and then Jesus. This, of course, did not hold until the Church threatened "excommunication" in the Sixth Century C.E. In the earliest story ISAIAH vii : 14 she is..."TO A WOMAN A CHILD WILL BE BORN."

First : To say that Ywh was speaking to Jesus Christ, according to orthodox Christian theological mythology when, in fact, Jesus Christ was no where around, even in terms of being a "WORD" until the Prophet Isaiah was to mention the coming of the "EMANUEL" in his allegorical prophecy - ISAIAH [or Isaia], Chapter vii, Verses 1 - 25 [See footnote on page 18 of this Volume] could be nothing more than an aspect of FAITH. But in "FAITH," as I understand the term,there should be some sort of rational posibility. Second: It certainly would have been that much easier for Ywh to had called another person and had him announce the arrival of Jesus Christ in the same manner as described by Isaiah.

While we are ending the second phase of the Hebrew GENESIS with the Prophet Isaiah, it is important to note that this outstanding Hebrew Prophet, himself, considered the indigenous Africans ["NEGROES, BLACKS, COLOUREDS, NIGGERS," etc.] of Ethiopia, East Africa to be of the greatest. He stated, according to ISAIAH, Chapter xviii, Verses 1 - 7:

> 3 [Ethiopia] Ah, land of buzzing insects, beyond the rivers of Ethiopia, 2
> sending ambassadors by sea, in papyrus boats on the waters! Go, swift messengers, to a nation tall and bronzed, to a people dreaded near and far, a nation strong and conquering, whose land is washed by rivers. All who inhabit the world, who dwell on earth, when the signal is raised on the mountain, look! When the trumpet blows, listen!
> 4 For thus says the Lord to me: "I will quietly look on from where I dwell, like the glowing heat of sunshine, like a cloud of dew at harvest
> time. 5 Before the vintage, when the flowering is ended, and the blooms are succeeded by ripening grapes, then comes the cutting of branches
> with pruning hooks and the discarding of the lopped-off shoots. 6 They
> shall all be left to the mountain birds of prey, and to the beasts in the land; the birds of prey shall summer on them and on them all the beasts of the earth shall winter.
> 7 Then will gifts be brought to the Lord of hosts from a people tall and bronzed, from a people dreaded near and far, a nation strong and conquering, whose land is washed by rivers, - to Mount Sion where dwells the name of the Lord of hosts.

Observe very carefully that "ETHIOPIA" is hundreds of miles south of Egypt; that its landmass is approximately 4,000 feet above mean sea level; and it is generally very hot in the day [to 110^0 F], but very cool at night [to 60 or 50^0 F]. Thus, again, I quote from ISAIAH, Chapter xviii, Verse 2 for the physical identification of the Ethiopians:

> "Go, swift messengers, to a nation [Ethiopia] of tall and bronzed [burnt skin or black] people."[1]

---

1. I differ very strongly with the English traslation of the Greek and Hebrew versions, as shown in the bracketed words I have inserted. "Bronze" is modern semantics to avoid the usual so-called "Negroes, Blacks," and even "Hamites."

Certainly Isaiah's racial description of the Ethiopians was no different than Herodotus description of the Egyptians a few generations later in ca. 457 or 450 B.C.E. Herodotus wrote:

> "The Colchians, Egyptians and Ethiopians have thick lips, broad nose, woolly hair, and they are burnt of skin...," etc.

I would certainly suggest that the chronology of Isaiah be carefully re-examined, as his prophecy was preached around ca. 718 - 717 B.C.E., which was during the XXIVth Dynasty of Nile Valley civilization. This was a period when Egypt, Nubia and Ethiopia were under the rule of an Ethiopian named Suten Kasta Men-xeper - Ra, Son of the Sun P-anxi [author's translation: King Kashta Men-xeper - God, Son of God Piankhi].[1]

The introduction of Ethiopia, East Africa into the prophecies of Isaiah is ideal, equally of Egypt, Northeast Africa; but it would have been geographically, socio-politically and religiously impossible for the Hebrew people of Isaiah's era [ca. 718 - 712 B.C.E.] not to have had contact with the Nubians who lived and ruled over the land and nation located between Egypt [at its North] and Ethiopia [at its South]. Once more the racial bigotry and all of its accompanying negrophobism that permeate the various translations, revisions, versions and general distortions of the OLD and NEW TESTAMENT by European and European-American so-called "scholars, theologians" and "academicians" have been, so far, equally victorious over the prophetic words of the Prophet Isaiah. Or, are we to believe that Ywh and Jesus Christ were equally as RACIST and RELIGIOUSLY BIGOTED as those of us who pretend to follow either, or both, when we write our own bigoted versions of the OLD and NEW TESTAMENT? The article on pages 69 and 70 shows how academia vasilates on Jesus' COLOR.

The answer to the distortions in the BOOK OF GENESIS [the first of the Five Books Of Moses] is based in the need for a completely new set of BOOKS for the religious direction of all who desire to be free of a Europeanized and Semiticized-Caucasoid lily-white blonde racial and religious bastardization of the African-Asian experiences of the ancient indigenous African and Asian peoples' ancestral glory. This would, of course, illiminate the need for Michaelangelo's image of a CAUCASIAN Jesus Christ[2] with Asian parents of the Hebrew religion - Joseph and Mary, and disciples, he painted in the Cisteen Chaple of St. Peter's Basillica for Pope Julius IInd during the Sixth Century C.E. But the fact that even "Negro Churches" would protest against this exposure should not cause any possible delay. If

---

1. The year ca. 718 - 717 B.C.E. is equivalent to ca. 701 - 702 B.C.E. in some of the modern chronological charts by "Western scholars."
2. Originally Africa's "Isis and Horus" or "Goddess of Fertility and Child" copied by Europeans as "The Black Madonna and Child" or "Mary and the Christ Child." See BLACK MAN OF THE NILE AND HIS FAMILY, pp. 124 - 126, 200, 373 - 379.

"TRUTH IS GODLINESS," and this is what all of us have been told, them we must assume that God [Ywh, Jesus, Al'lah, Damballah Ouedo, Ngai, etc.], equally, wants "TRUTH" to prevail over "WHITE RACISM" in the Book Of Genesis used in the synagouges, churches and mosques to this very day; the same institutions that teach about a different kind of...

> "IN THE BEGINNING [Genesis] WAS THE WORD [Voodum]; BLESSED BE THE WORD; AND THE WORD WAS HEARD BY ALL: SO MAY IT ALWAYS."[1]

But now we are forced by current archaeological findings to re-examine Africa for another aspect of GENESIS; and again Africa proves to be MOTHER OF THE NEW GENESIS. Yet, we find that this much more ancient GENESIS took place along the Great Lakes of Central East Africa and their surroundings in Ethiopia, Kenya, Tanzania, Zimbabwe [colonial Rhodesia], Zambia, Zaire, etc., and not along the banks of the Tigris and Euphrates River of Asia like the GENESIS of belief ; this GENESIS being the evolutionary development of mankind over millions of years in Alkebu-lan [Africa]. Yet, once again, the indigenous Africans are being extracted from another of their GENESIS, and Europeans substituted in their place. Thus we note the graphical presentation of the origin and development of evolutionary man on the following page of this Volume by "one of the United States of America's outstanding authority in the field of archaeology" - Professor J. Desmond Clark. As we examined Clark's graphic "[conjectural]" negrophobia very carefully, particularly his "MODERN MAN," less the "NEGRO" he forgot to show, in what he prefers to call "THE EMERGENCE OF MAN IN AFRICA [conjectural]."[2] Of course his "NEGRO," in the center of Africa no less, followed his "MODERN MAN" [Caucasian and/or Semite] in time of their GENESIS in Africa. However, the expertly tactfull RACIST myth injected into the term "MODERN MAN," in place of the much more blatent "MEMBER OF THE GREAT WHITE RACE," is also apparent here, just as it was expressly specified in Lothrop S. Stoddard's THE RISING TIDE OF COLOR and M.D.W. Jeffreys' "THE NEGRO ENIGMA."[3] For example, Stoddard wrote on page 90 of his work the following:[4]

> From the first glance we see that, in the Negro, we are in the presence of a being different profoundly not merely from the white man but also from those human types which we discovered in our surveys of the brown and

---

1. From the teachings of Voodum - God of the VOODOO religion. Words in brackets inserted for the purpose of clarity only. Mandkind's GENESIS are as varied as they are religions.
2. In: HORIZON AFRICAN HISTORY, pp. 24 - 25.
3. In: WEST AFRICAN REVIEW, September 1951 issue.
4. L.S. Stoddard, THE RISING TIDE OF COLOR, New York, 1928

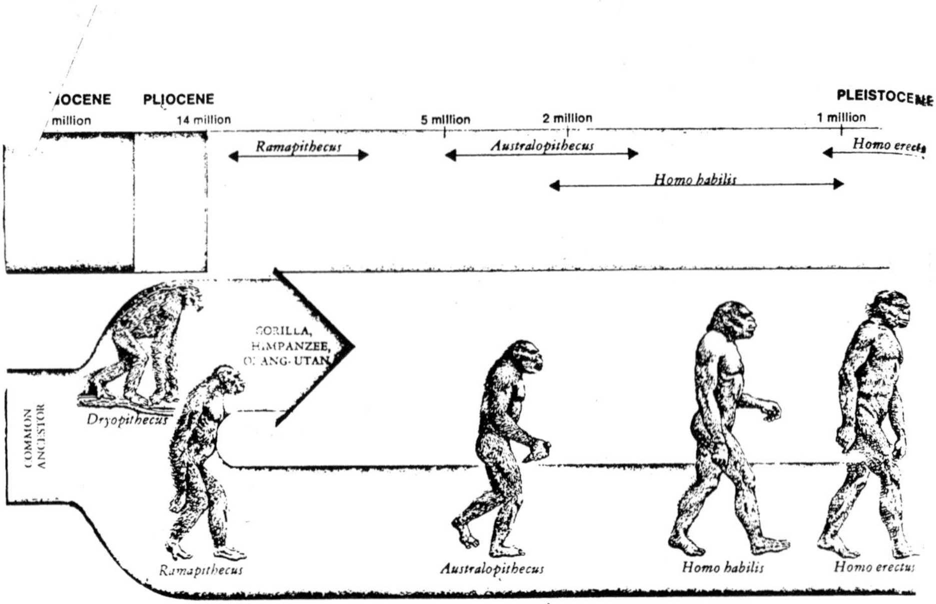

[continued below]

THE EMERGENCE OF MAN IN AFRICA *(conjectural)*[1]

[continued from above]

1. See J. Desmond Clark's "The Emergence Of Man In Africa [conjectural]," in: THE HORIZON AFRICAN HISTORY, pp. 24 - 25; GENESIS i : 1 - 10 on pages 6, 7 and 9 of this Volume. Is it not strange that professor Clark did not show his "NEGRO" along with his "MODERN MAN?" On the evolutionary scale of the above graph his "Homo sapiens sapiens" [white or Caucasian] "modern man" arrived some "11,000" years in Africa before his "NEGRO." This refutes Dr. Stoddard's position of the ["negro"] "...being differing profoundly not merely from the white man but also from those human types which we discovered in our surveys of the brown and yellow worlds" [See pp. 21 and 23 of this Volume].

> yellow worlds. The black man is, indeed, sharply differentiated from the other branches of mankind. His outstanding qualities is super-abundant animal vitality. In this he easily surpasses other races. To it he owes his intense emotionalism. To it, again, is due his extreme fecundity, the Negro being the quickest of the breeders. This abounding vitality shows in many other ways, such as the Negro's ability to survive harsh conditions of slavery under which other races have succumbed. Lastly, in the ethnic crossings, the Negro strikingly displays his prepotency, for black blood, once entering a human stock, seems never really bred out again.

On pages 96 and 97 of the same book Stoddard wrote:

> "...Certainly, all white men, whether professing Christians or not, should welcome the success of missionary efforts in Africa. The degrading fetishism and demonology which sum up the native pagan cults cannot stand, and all Negroes will some day be either Christian or Moslems. In so far as he is Christianized, the Negro's savage instincts will be restrained and he will be disposed to acquiesce in white tutelege. In so far as he is Islamized, the Negro warlike propensities will be inflamed, and he will be used as the tool of Arab Pan-Islamism seeking to drive the white man from Africa and make the continent his very own."

Following our notation of the graphical presentation by professor J. Desmond Clark on the origin and development [emergence] of man in Africa.. we must remain with the thought that his "MODERN MAN" preceded even the usually stereotyped "NEGRO SOUTH OF THE SAHARA" by at least "11,000" years in what men like himself still call "DARKEST AFRICA."

Obviously Stoddard's WHITE RACISM, which is grounded in the Sixth Century C.E. obnoxious plagiarization of GENESIS by European "Jewish scholars" on the story about Noah and his sons, is equally carried forward in the presentation by professor Clark and others before him... such as anthropologist James Henry Breasted, colonial imperialist Henry Morton Stanley, colonialist historian Sir Harry H. Johnston, imperialist masters of genocide King Leopold II of Belgium, Queen Victoria and Captain [Lord] F. Lugard of Britain, also American slavery apologist historian Ulrich B. Phillips.

As you have already seen in BLACK MAN OF THE NILE AND HIS FAMILY,[1] equally in CULTURAL GENOCIDE IN THE BLACK AND AFRICAN STUDIES CURRICULUM,[2] everything suggestive of an "AFRICAN GENESIS" upon which European and European-American ["WESTERN"] Civilization depends is eventually designated by European and European-American "educators" of every discipline... "THE WORKS OF MODERN MAN" [Caucasian, Semite, etc.]. And if such words are not used, then we are bombarded with pictures like

---

1. By Yosef ben-Jochannan
2. Ibid.

Maurice Wilson's "ZINJANTHROPUS BOISIE" [an African fossil-man unearthed in Tanzania, Central - East Africa] I have included on this and the following page.

CHARACTERISTICS OF ZINJANTHROPUS BOISIE 1

Fossils Trace Man Back 600,000 Years In Gorge in Africa

LEOPOLDVILLE, Belgian Congo, Aug. 23 (Reuters)—Human fossils about 600,000 years old—possibly the earliest known trace of man—have been found in Tanganyika.

Dr. Louis S. B. Leakey, a prominent anthropologist, said that his wife, also an anthropologist, had found the fossil among animal remains in th Oldoway Gorge in Tanganyika, July 17.

Dr. Leakey, 56 years old, a British expert on East African anthropology, has searched for many years to prove his belie that man originated in Africa. He is curator of the Corydon Museum of Natural History in Nairobi, Kenya.

Dr. Leakey reported his wife's find to the Pan-African Congress of Prehistory here yesterday. Sixty delegates from fifteen countries, including the United States, are at the congress.

Crude tools were found with the fossils, suggesting some form of human culture, Dr Leakey said. He said a reconstruction of the bones showed a skull that was estimated to date from the second half of the Pleistocene geological era 600.000 years ago.

N.Y.Times.Aug.24,1959

Palate and teeth of "boise" (below) compared with those of an Australian indiginous man (so-called"aborigine").

National Geographic Magazine, Sept. 1960, has a picture of one skull, and quotes Prof. Leakey as saying that it was that of the first tool-making human ; and that the discoveries "strongly support Charles Darwin's prophecy that Africa would prove to have been the birthplace of mankind."

Prof. Leakey has since discovered a still older skull "considerably more than 600,000 years old." With it were other human relics, one of them a child (New York Times, Feb. 25, 1961).

N. Y. Times, Aug. 24, 1959.

• • •

The age of the skulls is now set at 1,750,000 years. (*New York Times*, July 23, 1961.)

Side view of skull

External construction of skull and face.

Front view of skull

Left: Reconstruction of the Rhodesian Man with the original skull

The skull was found at Broken Hill Rhodesia, almost in the heart of Africa with 160 feet of packed above it

1. See Y. ben-Jochannan, BLACK MAN OF THE NILE AND HIS FAMILY, pp. 73 - 98. This article made me recall T.W. Doane's BIBLE MYTHS AND THEIR PARALLELS IN OTHER RELIGIONS, pp. 5 - 6, where he quotes from Max Muller's THE SCIENCE OF RELIGION, p. 302, with respect to the Malagassy Africans' CREATION" story; thusly:

> "...the first man was created of the dust of the earth, and was placed in a garden, where he was subject to none of the ills which now affect morality; he was also free from all bodily appetites, and through surrounded by delicious fruit and limpid streams yet felt no desire to taste of the fruit or to quaff the water. The Creator, had, moreover, strictly forbid him either to eat or to drink. The great enemy, however, came to him, and painted to him, in glowing colors, the sweetness of the apple, and the lusciousness of the date, and the succulence of the orange."

Dr. Delitzsch, writing of the Persian legend, saw a corallory to the above last sentence. The legend states:

> "Innumerable attendants of the Holy One keep watch against the attempts of Ahriman, over the tree Hom, which contains in itself the power of the resurrection." [See "The Fruit and Soap of this 'Tree of Life' begat immortality,"in Bonwick, EGYPTIAN BELIEF, p. 240].

RECONSTRUCTION OF FOSSIL-MAN[1]

(Top) Reconstruction of Zinjanthropus boisie (African fossil-man)

(Bottom) Skull of Zinjanthropus boisie unearthed in Bed I of Ol Olduvai Gorge, Tanganyika, by Dr's. L.S. & M. Leakey.

Full figure attempt by Maurice Wilson

(Top) A sculptured attempt at reconstructing Neanderthal man (European fossil-man).

(Bottom) An attempt in paint. Both by Maurice Wilson.

---

1. See Y. ben-Jochannan, BLACK MAN OF THE NILE AND HIS FAMILY, pp. 73 - 98. The above pictures remind me of the following from Smith's CHALDEAN ACCOUNT OF GENESIS New York, p. 91 on the "Tree Of Life" and the "Sacred Grove" [Eden] I extracted from Doane's BIBLE MYTHS..., etc. Smith wrote about the following Fig. No. 1:

> "One striking and important specimen of early type in the British Museum collection, has two figures sitting one on each side of a TREE, holding out their hands to the fruit, while at the back of one [THE WOMAN] is scratched a SERPENT. We know well that in these early sculptures none of these figures were chance devices, but all represented events, or supposed events, and figures in their legends; thus it is evident that a form of the story of the Fall, similar to that of Genesis, was known in early times in Babylonia."

Fig No 1

Unfortunately Jewish, Christian and Moslem parishoners are in danger of missing the entire story of this aspect of the SCIENTIFIC AFRICAN GENESIS. First: Because they are even denied their THEOLOGICAL GENESIS that is rooted in the philosophical and spiritual teachings of the indigenous Africans of the MYSTERIES SYSTEM of the Nile Valley High-Cultures at the Grand Lodge of Luxor, much of which we can still find in the following works left us [yet stored in Museums and Libraries all over Europe, Great Britain and the United States of America]- BOOK OF THE COMING FORTH BY DAY AND BY NIGHT,[1] PYRAMID TEXT, COFFIN TEXT, OSIRIAN DRAMA, NEGATIVE CONFESSIONS,[2] etc. Second: Because they are constantly being denied their rights of knowing the evolutionary side of GENESIS without being subjected to the constant threat of "His Satanic Majesty" - the DEVIL" - whom preachers of doom for a satanical GOD created and approved in the name of Ywh, Jesus Christ, Al'lah; and, whose main claim to fame is a vicious temper that will one day make him cook men, women and infants like frankfurters over a red-hot furnace which they have designated" THE ETERNAL HELL FIRE." Never the less the AFRICAN GENESIS, whether spiritual or evolutionary in its reality, remains indigenous to "Mother Alkebu-lan" [Africa of the Greeks and Romans that renamed it so] and her indigenous sons and daughters - the so-called "NEGROES, BANTUS, NILOTS, PYGMIES, HOTTENTOTS, BUSHMEN," etc. or plain old "AFRICANS SOUTH OF THE SAHARA." And no amount of European and European-American academic 'CAUCASIANIZING, SEMITICIZING' or "MODERNIZING' can change this fact; not even professor J. Desmond Clark's "MODERN MAN [Conjectural]"...negrophobia.

Judaism, Christianity and Islam, not withstanding, must deal with these two GENESIS: [a] the spiritual process based upon "theological faith" developed among the Nile Valley Africans and; [b] the "evolutionary process" that took place among the indigenous Great Lakes Africans ["BLACKS, NEGROES," etc.] of the heart of central East Africa. Unfortunately economic and socio-political considerations on the part of those who are in control of religious expressions and the socio-political and economic livelihood of everyone within the so-called "WESTERN WORLD" and its colonial outposts must change first. The irony of it is that any change at all will bring forth untold racial and religious strifes, as mankind in the "WESTERN WORLD" has indicated no desire for everlasting survival on the Planet Earth, at least from our present pattern of racism and religious bigotry to date.

---

1. Also called "Egyptian Book Of The Dead," as translated by E.A. Wallis Budge, London, 1885, with its accompanying "Papyrus Of Ani."

2. See "Extracts of the Negative Confessions" on p. 46 of this Volume, with comments on pp. 45 - 47.

Yes! Let us truly examine the GENESIS of mankind without prejudice; and let the African fossil-man we have already examined on pages 24 and 25, including the pictures of the fragments of the fossil-head on pages 27 and 28 following, all of which I have documented in detail for you on pages 40, 41 and 104 - 109 of CULTURAL GENOCIDE IN THE BALCK AND AFRICAN STUDIES CURRICULUM, equally in BLACK MAN OF THE NILE AND HIS FAMILY, Chapter II: Prehistoric Homosapiens, Pages 73 - 98, speak. They must be compared with the JUDAEO-CHRISTIAN-ISLAMIC "GENESIS" without prejudice - religiously or scientifically; and...

"THE TRUTH SHALL SET YOU [us] FREE."

NEW YORK, FRIDAY, NOVEMBER 10, 1972

Skull Pushes Back Man's Origin[1]

By WALTER SULLIVAN

Ancient bones found in Africa have been assembled into a skull that may extend man's immediate ancestry back more than one million years earlier than previously believed.

The fragments, making up a skull with striking resemblances to that of modern man, were found in a layer of material that had been deposited about 2.6 million years ago.

Richard Leaky, co-leader of the expedition that found the bones, said the skull seemed to displace two other man-like creatures widely thought to represent the early stages in man's development.

One of them, a beetle-browed type known as Homo erectus, lived far more recently—about a million years ago—yet is less like modern man than the newly found skull.

The other reputed ancestor, Australopithecus, an ape-like "man" that walked relatively erect, lived 2.5 to 3 million years ago. It now appears to have been a contemporary of the more modern-looking type, rather than ancestral to the men of today.

"There is now clear evidence that in eastern Africa a large-brained, truly upright and bipedal form of the genus Homo existed contemporaneously with Australopithecus more than 2.5 million years ago," Mr. Leakey said.

© National Geographic Society/Bob Campbell

Richard Leakey with the skull, found in fragments

The new find was made in a desert region on the east side of Lake Rudolph, one of the chain of elongated lakes within the rifts of East Africa. In the last two years the site has produced a rich harvest of stone tools, considered to be the oldest known artifacts of man.

According to Dr. J. Desmond Clark, professor of anthropology at the University of California at Berkeley, whose former student, Dr. Glynn Isaac, was co-leader of the expedition with Mr. Leakey, the tools lay within a layer of congealed volcanic ash, or tuff, known to be about 2.6 million years old.

Dr. Isaac is in Kenya, but Dr. Clark was reached by tele-

Continued on Page 16, Column 1

1. See BLACK MAN OF THE NILE AND HIS FAMILY, pp. 73 - 98; also CULTURAL GENOCIDE IN THE BLACK AND AFRICAN STUDIES CURRICULUM, pp. 104 - 120.

Skull Pushes Back Man's Origins One Million Years[1]

Continued From Page 1, Col. 5

phone in Berkeley. The skull, he said, was originally buried by this ash layer and so must be at least as old.

The skull had been crushed to hundreds of fragments that were found, eroding on a slope, and have been pieced together by Dr. Maeve Leakey, Richard Leakey's wife. Mr. Leakey is the son of the late Louis S. B. Leakey, pioneer collector, in this region, of fossil remnants of man's earliest ancestors.

The find was announced yesterday by the National Geographic Society, which, with the National Science Foundation and the National Museums of Kenya, provided support for the Lake Rudolf excavations. It quoted Mr. Leakey as saying:

"While the skull is different from our own species, Homo sapiens, it is also different from all other known forms of early man and thus does not fit into any of the presently held theories of human evolution."

Cranial Volume Large

Mr. Leakey, who is administrative director of the National Museums of Kenya, said the cranial volume of this skull was large, indicating a brain size of 800 cubic centimeters.

By contrast the cranial volume of this early man's contemporary, Australopithecus, was less than 500 cubic centimeters, he said. That of modern man is some 1,500 cubic centimeters.

Unresolved is the relationship of the new find to Homo habilis, whose skull fragments were found in Olduvai Gorge, 500 miles south of the Lake Rudolf site, in a layer 1.75 million years old. The hand bones of this species suggested a dexterity approaching that of modern man, and Dr. Clark suspects the new find may be an earlier form of Homo habilis.

However, the brain chamber of the latter was only about 656 cubic centimeters, compared to Mr. Leakey's estimate of 800 for the newly pieced-together skull. The subsequent Homo erectus, represented by Java Man, Peking Man and various forms in Europe and Africa, had a brain volume from 935 to 1,225 cubic centimeters.

Whereas Homo erectus had the extremely heavy brow bone that continued to be typical of the early cave dwellers of Europe, as well as a thick jaw bone, these features seem to be far less prominent in the new, though much earlier, skull.

"The whole shape of the brain case is remarkably reminiscent of modern man, lacking the heavy and protruding eyebrow ridges and thick bone that are characteristic of Homo Erectus known from young deposits in both Africa and Asia," Mr. Leakey said.

Thigh Bones Found

Also found at the site were two intact thigh bones from other individuals as well as parts of the lower leg (tibula and fibula). They indicate that at this stage man had already graduated from the stooped, loping gait inherited from his arboreal ancestors. Previous studies, Mr. Leakey said, had led to the belief that this graduation occurred much later.

The leg specimens, he added, "have astounded anatomists and other scientists because they are practically indistinguishable from the same bones of modern man."

Dating of the African finds has been done by three methods. In one, a sample of volcanic debris or other material associated with the find is analyzed to determine the extent to which a radioactive form of potassium has decayed into argon gas. This indicates the time since the material erupted at high temperature.

Another method measures how long a specimen containing uranium has been in existence through the number of tracks left in it by the radioactive decay of that uranium.

The third technique uses the known timetable of reversals in the earth's magnetic field over the last few million years as a time scale. When lava cools, after eruption, it becomes imprinted with the direction of the earth's magnetism at the time of cooling. Under favorable circumstances determination of the magnetism in a specimen can be fitted to the timetable of field reversals to obtain the age of a lava flow associated with human remains.

Specimens from the African rift valleys have been dated with particular confidence because volcanic activity there has been frequent, burying the specimens in layers that could be dated by one or all three of these methods.

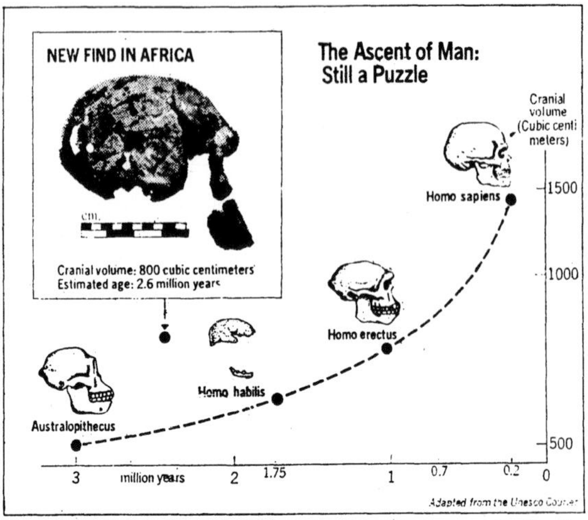

The gradual evolution of man's brain has been represented as a progression from the skull of Australopithecus to Homo sapiens. This progression is challenged by the recent discovery (inset) of an ancient skull near Lake Rudolf in Africa.

The New York Times/Nov. 10, 1972

1. The above reminds me of the following from Doane's BIBLE MYTHS, p. 2 footnote: "The geologist reckons not by days or by years; the whole six thousand years, which were until lately looked on as the sun of the world's age, are to him but as a unit of measurement in the long succession of past ages." [Sir John Lubbock responding to the story of "Creation"].

BIBLIOGRAPHY FOR LECTURE No. I

[Books listed according to chronological order of appearance in the text]

Y. ben-Jochannan, AFRICAN ORIGINS OF THE MAJOR "WESTERN RELIGIONS, New York, 1972
------------- AFRICA: MOTHER OF "WESTERN CIVILIZATION," New York, 1971
------------- BLACK MAN OF THE NILE, New York, 1969
------------- BLACK MAN OF THE NILE AND HIS FAMILY, New York, 1972
HOLY TORAH [Old Testament; Confraternity Version, Guild Press, New York, 1961]
HOLY BIBLE [New Testament; Revised Standard Version, The World Publishing Company, Cleveland, Ohio, 1962; and all other Versions]
HOLY QURAN [Sheik Muhammad Ashraf Pakistan, 1938; and all other Versions]
Count C.F. Volney, RUINS OF EMPIRE, New York, 1950 [originally published in French in Paris, 1792, and translated into English in London, 1800?]
Wm. Turner, HISTORY OF PHILOSOPHY, New York
Sir E.A. Wallis Budge, EGYPTIAN BOOK OF THE DEAD, London, 1885
------------ PAPYRUS OF ANI, London, 1885
PAPYRUS OF NESI-ANSU, London Museum of Natural History
ARCHAEOLOGIA, Vol. LII, London, 1891
I. Bruckner, CRITICAL HISTORY OF PHILOSOPHY, New York
H.S. Lewis, MYSTICAL LIFE OF JESUS, New York
C. H. Vail, ANCIENT MYSTERIES, New York
A. Besant, ESOTORIC CHRISTIANITY, New York
M. Muller, MYTHOLOGY OF EGYPT, New York,
G.G.M. James, STOLEN LEGACY, New York, 1954
Report of the Fourth Meeting of the Australasian Association for the Advancement of Science, Hobart, 1893
R. P. Trilles, "Les pygmees de la foret equatoriale," Paris, 1933
L. Froebenius, "Die altantische Gotterlechre," Atlantis, 1926, Vol. 10
"Book Of The Knowing How God Came Into Being" [in: EGYPTIAN HIERATIC PAPYRI, The British Museum, London, 1910]
K. Sethe, AMUN, London, 1909
BABYLONIAN TALMUD [Sixt Century A.D. Version by European rabbis and Talmudists]
R. Graves and R. Patai, HEBREW MYTHS, New York, 1964
L.S. Stoddard, THE RISING TIDE OF COLOR, New York, 1928
M.D.W. Jeffreys, "The Negro Enigma" [in: THE HIGHWAY, Sept. issue, 1951]
J. Desmond Clark, "The Emergence of Man in Africa [conjectural]"... [in: THE HORIZON AFRICAN HISTORY, New York, 1971]
Y. ben-Jochannan, CULTURAL GENOCIDE IN THE BLACK AND AFRICAN STUDIES CURRICULUM, New York, 1973
T.W. Doane, BIBLE MYTHS AND THEIR PARALLELS IN OTHER RELIGIONS, London, 1888
M. Muller, THE SCIENCE OF RELIGION, New York
L. Bonwick, EGYPTIAN BELIEF, New York,
C. Smith, CHALDEAN ACCOUNT OF GENESIS, New York
PYRAMID TEXT [ed. by K. Sethe in: Die altaegyptischen Pyramidentexte, Liepzig, 1908-22]
COFFIN TEXT [ed. by A. deBuck and A.H. Gardiner, Chicago, Ill., 1935 - 38, 4 vols.]
OSIRIAN DRAMA [in: E.A.Wallis Budge's transl. of "Book Of The Dead" and "Papyrus Of Ani]
NEGATIVE CONFESSION [Ibid]

Note: All newspaper clippings are listed under "ILLUSTRATIONS."

PRELUDE TO EXODUS

Like Genesis, the BOOK OF EXODUS [also known as the "Second Book Of Moses"] has been interpreted and reinterpreted over and over by Europeans and European-Americans by the thousands in order to exclude many books and teachings, among which is one of the very important segment of the peoples it was originally written about...the so-called "NEGROES" or "BLACK PEOPLE" [Africans]. Yet more than eighty percent of the entire drama of the story called "EXODUS" took place in Africa before there was a book of said name. Thus it should not surprise anyone, or should it, that the people who played the major roles in this drama were, for the most part, Africans like the millions upon millions of African-Americans and African-Caribbeans one meets daily in the Americas and the Caribbeans, all of whom are no different than their relatives in the "Motherland" - Alkebu-lan [Africa or Afrika] were, and still are.

You, as students, by this juncture, understand that it is not coincidental when the term "JEW" or "SEMITE" is used here in these United States of America as a member of the so-called "CAUCASIAN" or "SEMITIC RACE" that is "WHITE" in color is visualized; and that said person, by virtue of his or her COLOR and RACE, is related to people in the bible who were solely of this "RACE" wherever the words "HEBREW, ISRAELITE" and/or "JEW" appear. Also, that it is only these "CAUCASIAN" or "SEMITIC PEOPLE" who are the ones entitled to share in the land presently called "ISRAEL," as descendants of the biblical "Jews" with Moses in the EXODUS. But the words "JEW" and "SEMITE" have absolutely nothing whatsoever to do with "CAUCASIAN" and "WHITE" any more so than with "MONGOLIAN" and "YELLOW" or "AFRICAN" and "BLACK." Why? Because there are "JEWS" and/or so-called "SEMITES" who are of all of the "RACES" and "COLORS" known to mankind today; and not one of them can claim any more authoritative [kosher] right to the original "HARIBU"[Hebrew, Israelite or Jew] by virtue of his or her "RACE" and/or "COLOR." Professor H. Fishberg made this fact very clear in his extensive work in which he challenged the "Jewish Race" myth.

In the first place; a "JEW" is supposedly anyone from the "TRIBE OF JUDAH" who worship Ywh [Jehovah or God] according to the teachings in the FIVE BOOKS OF MOSES [Holy Torah or Old Testament]. This fact is irrespective of the dictates of certain people who control most of the branches of what is today called "TALMUDIC JUDAISM;" those who equally proclaimed that:

"IN ORDER TO QUALIFY AS A JEW ONE'S MOTHER HAS TO BE A JEW."

1. M. Fishberg's, THE JEWS, London, 1911.

But there is no such requirement listed in any of the FIVE BOOKS OF MOSES. And if it was so listed; what about the "Jewish child" whose mother had him or her for one of the invaders of Israel from Egypt, Ethiopia, Nubia, Persia, Assyria, Turkey, Greece, Rome, etc. who was not a "Jew?"

Second: A "SEMITE" is anyone whose culture include a national language under the designation of "SEMITIC LANGUAGE GROUP," which could be any of the languages of the so-called "MIDDLE EAST" that was formerly comprised of parts of Africa, Asia and Europe at the eastern limits of the Mediterranean Sea according to the maps I have shown on page 35 of this Volume.

In otherwords, there is no such thing as a "JEWISH RACE" or "JEWISH COLOR;" equally as there is no 'CHRISTIAN, MOSLEM' or 'YORUBA RACE' and/or 'COLOR.' Yet, there are those whose future political and economic "SUPERIORITY" depend upon the perpetuation of the myth of a "JEWISH" or "SEMITIC RACE." And with said alleged "RACIAL STOCK" established in one's mind, it is very easy to brainwash such a person with the racist myth of an AFRICAN-LESS [black-less] EXODUS that supposedly took place in Africa's Ta-Merry [Kamt, Kimit, etc.] - which the Hebrews renamed "EGYPT" in their mythology and allegory about "Noah and his sons" folk-lore in Genesis. Of course this particular aspect of "Western Civilization's" white racism was not always a part of Hebrew mythology, as it was not too very long ago that European and European-American [WHITE] Jews were not able to participate in many aspects of the socio-political life "...FOR CAUCASIANS [whites] ONLY...," even to register as "WHITE" in many municipalities throughout the United States of America and Europe.

The "PURE WHITE" image of the biblical Hebrews is perpetuated by omission and commission on the part of rabbinical scholars, most of whom make no effort in informing their parishoners and the general public at large of the thousands of BLACK Jews [Falashas or Beta Israelis] of Ethiopia, East Africa, and the BROWN Jews [Yemenites][1] of Yemen, Western Asia. They did not tell their parishoners that many of the BLACK and BROWN Jews have equally migrated to the Americas and the Caribbean like European [WHITE] Jews did; and that many more have migrated even to Israel[2] - where they are suffering social segregation tion similar to the vast majority of the African people of the United States of America. Thus, by virtue of said ignorance of these facts, the vast majority of the people of the United States

1. All of the Yemenite Jews in Yemen were removed to Israel shortly after its founding.
2. See page 56 of this Volume for pictures of the Falasha, and page 60 for African-American "Israelites" [the so-called "Black Jews"].

of America, black and white, Jew and non-Jew, alike, are misled to believe that all of the "BLACK JEWS" of the world came by way of the few "NEGRO CONVERTS" to European and European-American "TALMUDIC [form of] JUDAISM." This image also perpetuates the AFRICAN-LESS and/or BLACK-LESS Exodus of the Hebrews from Africa into Asia which, supposedly, took place during the reign of Pharaoh Rameses II of the XIXth Dynasty [ca. 1298 - 1232 B.C.E.] of the Egyptian Empire. Because of these facts, and in order to properly follow the chronological details of the bible, I have included the following calendar below and a chart of the dynasties on page 33 following.

At this juncture, I must remind you that up to this period in the "BLACK EXPERIENCE" there were no Europeans [Caucasians, Semites, Indo-European Aryans, etc.] mentioned in Alkebu-lan's [Africa's] history, Egypt being a part thereto; and that the Greeks - the first of the Europeans to become "civilized" - were not yet known as a national entity in world history; thus the name "AFRICA" was not yet in use, but instead "ALKEBU-LAN."[1]

DIVISIONS OF THE 4,100 B. C. E. NILE YEAR CALENDAR [2] USED BY THE INDIGENOUS AFRICAN HIGH-PRIESTS FOR THEIR CALCULATIONS OF THE PERIODS OF THEIR HISTORY.

Akhet, season of inundation.	*Peret*, springtime, appearance of crops.	*Shemu*, summer.
1. Thoth. **or** *tepy* January I	5. Tybi. May I	9. Pachons. September I
2. Paophi. February II	6. Mechir. June II	10. Payni. October II
3. Hathor. March III	7. Phamenoth. July III	11. Epiphi. November III
4. Choiak. April IIII	8. Pharmouthi. August IIII	12. Mesore December IIII

12 Months, 365 1/4 Days, 3 Seasons of 4 Months each: AKHET (Season of Inundation), PERET (Springtime), and SHENU (Summer).

1. See BLACK MAN OF THE NILE AND HIS FAMILY, p. xxvi.
2. Ibid., p. 130

DATES OF EGYPTIAN DYNASTIES BY EUROPEAN "AUTHORITIES IN EGYPTOLOGY" COMPARED TO MANETHO'S ORIGINAL WORKS[1]

Period or DYNASTY	Manetho (280 B.C) DATE	Champollion-Figeac (?A D) DATE	Lepsius (1858AD) DATE	Brugsh (1877AD) DATE	Mariette (?AD) DATE
	First Book				
I	9K, 253Y	5,867*	3,892*	4,400*	5,004*
II	9K, 302Y	5,615	3,639	4,133	4,751
III	9K, 214Y	5,318	3,338	3,966	4,449
IV	8K, 284Y	5,121	3,124	3,733	4,235
V	9K, 248Y	4,673	2,840	3,566	3,951
VI	6K, 203Y	4,225	2,744	3,300	3,703
VII	70K, 0Y, 70D	4,222	2,592	3,100	3,500
VIII	27K, 146Y	4,147	2,522	?	3,500
IX	19K, 409Y	4,047	2,674**	?	3,358
X	10K, 185Y	3,947	2,565**	?	3,249
XI	192K, 2300Y, 70D	3,762	2,423	?	3,064
XII	7K, 160Y	3,703	2,380	?	2,851
XIII	?	3,417	2,136	2,235	?
XIV	76K, 184Y	3,004	2,167	?	2,398
XV	?	2,520	2,101	?	2,214
XVI	32K, 518Y	2,270	1,842	?	?
XVII	86K, 151Y	2,082	1,684	?	?
XVIII	16K, 263Y	1,822	1,581	1,700	1,703
	Second Book				
XIX	7K, 209Y	1,473	1,443	1,400	1,462
XX	12K, 135Y	1,279	1,269	1,200	1,288
XXI	7K, 130Y	1,101	1,091	1,100	1,110
XXII	9K, 126Y	971	961	966	980
XXIII	4K, 28Y	851	787	766	810
XXIV	1K, 6Y	762	729	733	721
XXV	3K, 40Y	718	716	700	715
XXVI	9K, 150Y, 6M	674	685	666	665
XXVII	8K, 124Y, 4M	524	525	527	527
XXVIII	1K, 6Y	404	525	?	406
XXIX	4K, 20Y, 4M	398	399	399	399
XXX	3K, 38Y	377	378	378	378
	Third Book				
XXXI***	?????????	399	340	340	340

1. See footnote Nos. 1 and 2 on page 32 of this Volume. The student will notice that the chronological dates given above by the four different European and European-American "authorities on Egypt" do not, for the most part, coincide with each other. I have taken time to point out the most flagrant of these differences to you, all of which you should take good care not to make any error in detailing your final papers. Make certain that you specify which one of the chronological dating processes you are using. This Lecture is based upon the original by High Priest Manetho's chronology.

* Note that the "authorities" disagree as much as 1,000 years difference.

** These dates only prove the extent to which Lepsius was confused in his work.

*** Manetho did not complete this dynasty's listing; he died before its termination in approximately ca. 324 B.C.E. He actually did not list it as a "DYNASTY."

The final DYNASTY, the XXXIst, was ended by the Romans when they turned Egypt into one of the North African PROVINCES of the Roman Empire following the conquest of Egypt in the year ca. 30 B.C.E. It is due to this factor that Christianity was later founded in Egypt by indigenous Africans of the "HEBREW RELIGION"- known as "THE NEW RELIGION."

You will recall that it was not until ca. 1675 B.C.E. that foreign [non-African] people ever ruled any part of Alkebu-lan, Asians called "Shepherd Kings of Beduina," whom certain academicians have since labeled:

"PEOPLE OF A SEMITIC RACE"

in their own racism, were the first. However, it must be noted that these Asians came into Ta-Merry[1] and parts of Lower Ta-Nehisi[2] during ca. 1675 B.C.E., which was during the reign of Pharaoh Sexeper-em-Ra, at the end of the XIVth Dynasty. Thus it was, from before the Ist Dynasty in ca. 3200 B.C.E. to the end of the XIVth Dynasty in ca. 1675 B.C.E., that all of Alkebu-lan [including Ta-Merry and Ta-Nehisi] was ruled and occupied by indigenous African [BLACK] people; and, not a single "SEMITE" or "HAMITE" on record existed in Alkebu-lan.[3] These facts are irrefutable, as there was no Moses to orally "PASS ON DOWN" his allegorical story about Noah and his sons in any "GREAT DELUGE" - as stated in his BOOK OF GENESIS.

Certainly, as students interested in the total "BLACK EXPERIENCE," you have never before given a thought to the fact that African people like those in the Harlems of the United States of America could have been involved in your biblical story that took place in their ancestors' homeland - Alkebu-lan [Africa]! Whereas, in the same instance, you have been taught to vizualize the entire drama of the history and people of North Alkebu-lan as a "European" or "Semitic Experience;" in otherwords... "WHITE." Yet none of the academicians, whose racism permeate the OLD and NEW Testament, could show how "WHITES" got there before "BLACKS" whom we were told for centuries Africa belongs to; or how it was possible for the "WHITES" from the Caucasus Mountains of Eastern Europe to have maintained their "lily-white Semitic-Caucasian racial stock" while living side by side with a "SAVAGE NEGRO SLAVE STATE" named "Nubia" adjacent to their "lily-white Egypt;" all of this is inspite of the fact that there was no natural or unnatural barrier of any kind that separated either group from the other. But, do you know what made you accept the "lily-white North Africa" squeel? All of us do, although we may not care to admit it. It stems from the bit of rabid racism and religious bigotry we were taught in the "CHOSEN PEOPLE" myth, along with the alleged "CURSE" Noah placed upon his own grandson - "CANAAN" and

---

1. The Jews called this land "EGYPT." See GENESIS x : 1 - 9.
2. One of the original names for the Sudan, including "ZETI" and "NUBIA."
3. See Y. ben-Jochannan, BLACK MAN OF THE NILE AND HIS FAMILY, pp. 1 - 18, 73 - 99, 127 - 250.

his descendants - the so-called "NEGRO [people] RACE."

Let us re-examine the SECOND BOOK OF MOSES, otherwise called "EXODUS," with respect to the two maps below on this page - the WORLD of Genesis and Exodus.

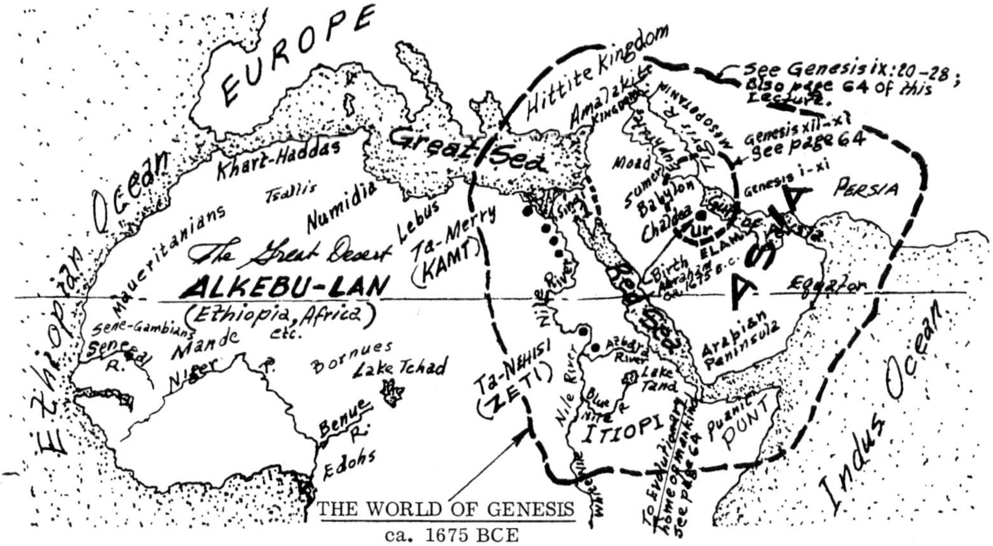

THE WORLD OF GENESIS
ca. 1675 BCE

THE WORLD OF EXODUS
ca. 1298 - 1232 BCE

The first contradiction we noticed is that Moses could not have crossed the "RED SEA" in an easterly direction of travel and enter the Sinai Peninsula without landing on the Western shore of the Arabian Peninsula first. And if the EXODUS did take place, it had to have been across the REED SEA [or Sea Of Reed]. The REED SEA was the only body of water they could have crossed that leads directly into the Sinai Peninsula at the easternmost part of the Egyptian Kingdom. The second point is that the Africans of Ta-Merry ruled the entire so-called "NEAR EAST" during the same period of the EXODUS, which was chronologically listed as sometime between ca. 1298 - 1232 B.C.E. Thus it would have been impossible for the Hebrews to have escaped the Egyptian armies when they entered the Sinai Peninsula that was, and still is, geographically part of Egypt, Northeast Alkebu-lan [Africa].

LECTURE No. II
RACISM AND THE AFRICAN JEWS WITH THE EXODUS INTO THE PROMISEDLAND: A JUDAEO-CHRISTIAN-ISLAMIC EXPERIENCE.

> "And it came to pass there was a wicked Pharaoh ruling over the land of Egypt who enslaved the Hebrew people...," etc.

This quotation is indicative of the manner in which the Hebrew writers recorded what they claimed "MOSES [orally] PASSED DOWN" to them through hundreds of other "GOD INSPIRED" intermediaries along the way. Of course we are expected to accept their "WORDS," as those in GENESIS, solely upon the fact that said writers stated they were "...<u>the inspired WORDS of GOD</u>." Thus solely upon the declaration of those Hebrew men, who were no different than any other man you and I meet every day we are alive, we are expected to believe whatever they wrote...IN BLIND "FAITH." Let us assume here for the sake of argument, just as we did in GENESIS, that these writers' story is as they have claimed..."THE INSPIRED WORDS OF GOD..." [Ywh]. Then we must also be ready to review the drama that caused Ywh to utter said"...INSPIRED WORDS..." to His "...INSPIRED WRITERS...."

The setting of our drama in the EXODUS had its genesis in a city called "SUCCOTH," which was geographically located in about the center of Egypt, Northeast Africa; the time, approximately ca. 1330 - 1340 - 1345 B.C.E.; and the occasion, the birth of an African named "MOSES."[1] However, like the story of the birth of Jesus Christ of Nazareth [the Christian God-head], there is no record of the romance, engagement and marriage between the parents of Moses, not even their names are given; and again like Jesus, he too disappeared...

---

1. EXODUS ii : 1 - 3. Mother"...a Levite..." is the only identification; father of the line of David; this is all there is about his immediate parents. His name means "FETCH FROM THE WATER" or " OF THE WATER."

even his physical remains - including bones and head-hair.

Using the terms "RACE, NATIONALITY" and/or "RELIGION" as the basis for Moses identification, only two of them his FIVE BOOKS used...viz-a-viz: NATIONALITY [Egyptian] and RELIGION [Hebrew or Israelite]. Thus we find in EXODUS, Chapter ii, Verses 15 - 22 the following:

> 15 Pharaoh, too, heard of the affair and sought to put him to death. But
> Moses fled from him and stayed in the land of Madian. 16 As he was seated
> there by a well, seven daughters of a priest of Madian came to draw water
> and fill the troughs to water their father's flock. 17 But some shepherds
> came and drove them away. Then Moses got up and defended them and water-
> ed their flock. 18 When they returned to their father Raguel, he said to them,
> "How is it you have returned so soon today?" 19 They answered, "An Egyptian
> saved us from the interference of the shepherds. He even drew water for us
> and watered the flock!" 20 "Where is the man?" he asked his daughters. "Why
> did you leave him there? Invite him to have something to eat." 21 Moses agreed
> to live with him, and the man gave him his daughter Sepphora in marriage. She
> bore him a son, whom he named Gersam; 22 for he said, "I am a stranger in a
> foreign land."

If any racial syndrome is to be drawn from this biblical drama it must be that Moses and his immediate family were BLACK; and their BLACKNESS pleased Ywh, to the extent that Ywh [the Jewish God] -

"...TURNED MARIAM [Moses' sister] INTO A LEPER..."

because of her objection to her brother - Moses - marrying a "CUSHITE" [Ethiopian][1] woman, according to the following from NUMBERS, Chapter xii, Verses 1 - 15:

> 1 [Jealousy of Aaron and Mariam] While they were in Haseroth, Mariam and
> Aaron spoke against Moses on the pretext of the marriage he had contracted
> with a Cushite woman. 2 They complained, "Is it through Moses alone that the
> Lord speaks? Does he not through us also?" And the Lord heard this. 3 Now,
> Moses himself was by far the meekest man on the face of the earth. 4 So at
> once the Lord said to Moses and Aaron and Mariam. "Come out, you three, to
> the Meeting Tent." And the three of them went. 5 Then the Lord came down in
> the column of cloud, and standing at the entrance of the tent, called Aaron and
> Mariam. 6 When both came forward, he said, "Now listen to the words of the
> Lord:
> Should there be a prophet among you, in visions will I reveal myself to him,
> in dreams will I speak to him; 7 not so with my servant Moses! 8 Throughout my
> house he bears my trust: 8 face to face I speak to him, plainly and not in riddles.
> The presence of the Lord he beholds. Why, then, did you not fear to speak
> against my servant Moses?"
>
> 9 [Mariam's Leprosy] So angry was the Lord against them that when he depart-
> ed, 10 and the cloud withdrew from the Tent, there was Mariam, a snow-white
> leper! When Aaron turned and saw her a leper, 10 "Ah, my Lord!" he said to

1. "CUSH" or "KUSH" was the Hebrews assigned to the Africans' AXUM, AXHUM" or ITIOPI. See GENESIS x : 6 for this fact dealing with the children of Ham and Canaan.

> Moses, "please do not charge us with the sin that we have foolishly committed." 12 Let her not thus be like the stillborn babe that comes forth from its mother's womb with its flesh half consumed." 13 Then Moses cried to the Lord, "Please, not this! Pray, heal her!" But the Lord answered Moses, "Suppose her father had spit in her face, would she not hide in shame for seven days? 14 Let her be confined outside the camp for seven days; only then may she be brought back." So Mariam was confined outside the camn for seven days, and the people did not start out again until she was brought back.
>
> 15 After that the people set out from Haseroth and encamped in the desert of Pharan.

Here, at least, we have the possiblity of a so-called "RACIAL INTERMARRIAGE;" that is providing Moses was something different to all of the other BLACK PEOPLE of his native Egypt - the so-called "CURSED NEGROES."

As we have noticed, there is no RACIAL identification stated **or** implied. This is only natural, for the obnoxious anxiety of "RACE" European and European-American "academicians" and "educators" created to support their colonialist and imperialist expansion over the WORLD, along with their ethnic supperiority over all other peoples, was not known in the same context by anyone of the ancient national groupings of the era of Moses. And we know that later on during the period of the PENTATEUCH, approximately ca. 800 - 700 B.C.E., there was no attempt at establishing a special "JEWISH RACE" European and European-American Jews have created. The attempt to create a "JEWISH [Semitic] RACE" moved professor George G.M. James to make the following observation about Moses in his major work - STOLEN LEGACY:[1]

> "...We are told not only by the bible, but also by the historian Philo, that Moses was an Initiate of the Egyptian Mysteries and became a Hierogrammat; learned in all the wisdom of the Egyptian people. This was only possible by proper initiation and gradual advancement, when evidence of fitness was demonstrated by the Neophyte."

Professor James is supported by the works of Philo, CHAERROMON: Jos. G. APION I, p. 32; Dr. James Hasting's BIBLE DICTIONARY [under the word "Pentateuch"]; and C.H. Vail's ANCIENT MYSTERIES; among many thousands more volumes, and by as many authors.

EXODUS, Chapter ii, Verses 1 - 10 identified Moses; his parentage; and his religion. It even states that the "PHARAOH'S DAUGHTER" was the person who saved the infant Moses from her own father's genocide against his fellow Africans - Egyptian Hebrews [Jews]. But the arrogance of the "INSPIRED [Hebrew] SCRIBES" did not allow the alleged "Pharaoh" [Haremheb or Rameses I] and his "daughter" to have names like their own Hebrew superstars -

---

1. G.G.M. James,'STOLEN LEGACY, p. 67. See H. Fishberg's THE JEW.

"MOSES," his brother "AARON," and his sister "MARIAM." In this same light, I suggest that you consult the story of the birth of Sargon of Akhad, who lived around ca. 2400 B.C.E. - more than 1000 years before the birth of Moses, for a very similar allegorical drama. But before you do this, you must question; how could... "THE PHARAOH'S DAUGHTER ADOPT HIM"... [Moses], according to EXODUS, Chapter ii, Verse 10, if he did not have the same countenance and color as all of the other African [Egyptian] boys of his era, particularly when her fahter did not lift his ban against every Jewish "MALE CHILD," according to EXODUS, Chapter i, Verses 8 - 22?

8 [The Oppression] Then a new king, who knew nothing of Joseph, came to
power. 9 He said to his subjects, "Look how numerous and powerful the
Israelite people are growing, more so than we ourselves! 10 Come, let us
deal shrewdly with them to stop their increase; otherwise, in time of war
they too may join our enemies to fight against us, and so leave our country."

11 Accordingly, taskmasters were set over the Israelites to oppress them
with forced labor. 12 Thus they had to build for Pharaoh the supply cities of
Phithom and Rameses. 13 Yet the more they were oppressed, the more they
multiplied and spread. 14 The Egyptians, then, dreaded the Israelites and
reduced them to cruel slavery, making life bitter for them with hard work
in mortar and brick and all kinds of field work - the whole cruel fate of slaves.

I have to interrupt at this point to make a major clarification on the possibility of a noted and most important figure like "Joseph, the greatest dreamer ever known in Egyptian history up until this period" in its thousands of years of existence before the birth of the first Israelite, Abraham; the man who caused the entire life-style of the entire empire to change because of the revelation of one of his dreams to Pharaoh Seti I - the father of Rameses II who supposedly "...knew nothing of Joseph,"...and had succeded his father ["...came to power"]. Growing up in his father's castle, and moving around with his father learning all that there was to know as the hier-apparent to the throne; how was it possible for Raneses II not to have met Joseph, muchless not even heard of him? May I also state that all of the "Major Pyramids" were already buillt by the end of the VIth Dynasty [ca. 2470 - 2270 B.C.E.]; and that the covering Verses 8 - 14 were during the period of the XIXth Dynasty [ca. 1555 - 1340 B.C.E.]. Thus the claim that "...the Israelites built the pyramids of Egypt...," which we find later on in the Torah, should be at least corrected to read - ' some of the pyramids of the XIXth Dynasty during the reign of Pharaoh Rameses II [ca. 1298 - 1232 B.C.E.]; and such is providing that this version of the Hebrews civil uprising did take place at all! Returning to our account of the alleged "OPPRESSION" we find the following:

15 [Command to the Midwives] The king of Egypt told the Hebrew midwives, one
of whom was called Sephra and the other Phua, 16 "When you act as midwives

for the Hebrew women and see them giving birth, if it is a boy, kill him; but if it is a girl, she may live." 17 The midwives, however, feared God; they did not do as the king of Egypt had ordered them, but let the boys live. So the king summoned the midwives and asked them, "Why have you acted thus, allowing the boys to live?" 19 The midwives answered Pharaoh, "The Hebrew women are not like the Egyptian women. They are robust and give birth before the midwife arrives." 20 Therefore God dealt well with the midwives. The people, too, increased and grew strong. 21 And because the midwives feared God, he built up families for them. 22 Pharaoh then commanded all his subjects, "Throw into the river every boy that is born to the Hebrews, but you may let all the girls live."

Either the recorders of this alleged act of the African who ruled Egypt during the period in question believe that all who read this story are totally ignorant; or they are showing total contempt for the "Pharaoh's" intelligence. Moreover; How ignorant could Rameses II have been in expecting that "..the Hebrew midwives..." would even see another Hebrew woman "... giving birth..." and then kill the child, "...if it is a boy?" I guess that in the name of God and the Judaeo-Christian-Islamic mystique we are to believe anything we read in the Bible as the "TRUTH", even when said teaching is contrary to the least bit of common sense, muchless scientific rationale. Yet there could be no doubt, according to Verses 8 - 22, that the Pharaoh's suppressive order was directed against the Hebrew people, most of whom up to this period had became the offsprings and descendants of their African "SLAVEMASTERS" [Blacks, Negroes, Bantus, etc.], which we can readily observe in the following from EXODUS, Chapter i, Verses 1 - 7:

1 [Jacob's Descendants in Egypt] These are the names of the sons of Israel who, accompanied by their households, migrated with Jacob into Egypt: 2 Ruben, Simeon, Levi and Juda; 3 Issachar, Zabulon and Benjamin; 3 Dan and Nephthali; 5 Gad and Aser. The total number of descendants.

6 Now Joseph and all his brothers and that whole generation of Jacob was seventy. Joseph was already in Egypt, died. 7 But the Israelites were fruitful and prolific. They became so numerous and strong that the land was filled with them.

It is obvious that at this period in question the Israelites or Hebrews [also "Jews"] were in Egypt as slaves, equally in Nubia. The only free ones during this period must have been those that travelled down to Ethiopia ["Kush"] long before the birth of Moses - who even married one of their number according to NUMBERS, Chapter xii, Verses 1 - 15, which we read on pages 37 and 38 of this Volume. These Jews are today called "FALASHAS" or FALASSA - the Ethiopian word for "STRANGER" in their national language called "Amharic," a few of whom I have shown on page 56 following. But we also noticed that even in the era of Joseph's entry into Africa two centuries before the birth of Moses, according to GENESIS, Chapter xxxvii, Verses 25 - 28, the Israelites themselves had already engaged in slavery when they sold Joseph to other slave traders; or are we to assume that this too was upon the direction of their own God - JEHOVAH - because of his preordained plan of things to had happened? It must be, for we teach that "...nothing happens without the pleasure of God." Thus we read:

> 25 [Joseph Sold into Egypt] Then they sat down to eat. Looking up, they saw a
> caravan of Ismaelites coming from Galaad, their camels laden with gum, balm,
> myrrh, with which they were on their way down to Egypt. 26 Then Juda said to
> his brothers, "What is to be gained by killing our brother and concealing his
> blood? 27 Let us sell him to the Ismaelites, and let us not lay hands on him; for
> he is our brother, our own flesh." His brothers agreed.
>
> 28 And when some Medianite traders passed by, they drew Joseph up out of the
> cistern; they sold him to the Ismaelites for twenty pieces of silver. And they
> took Joseph to Egypt.

There is no doubt that the recorders of the past could not make up their minds whether or not the people they were speaking about were - "HEBREWS, ISRAELITES" or "GOD'S CHOSEN PEOPLE;" nor whether they were "EGYTIAN SLAVES" or "SUBJECTS." They were equally confused if they were referring to "ISMAELITES" [the descendants of Abraham's first child] or "MEDIANITES" [people of the nation of whom Moses later on married one of the daughter of the High-Priest Raquel]. As for the Israelites, Hebrews or "Jews" being slavemasters following this period I refer you to the following from EXODUS, Chapter xxi, Verses 1 - 21, of which I will only quote from Verses 1 - 7 here; thus:

> 1 "Now these are the ordinances which you shall set before them. 2 When you
> buy a Hebrew slave, he shall serve six years, and in the seventh he shall go out
> free, for nothing. 3 If he comes in single, he shall go out single; if he comes in
> married, then his wife shall go with him. 4 If his master gives him a wife and
> she bears him sons or daughters, the wife and her children shall be her master's
> and he shall go out alone. 5 But if the slave plainly says, 'I love my master, my
> wife and my children; I will not go out free,' 6 then his master shall bring him to
> God, and he shall bring him to the door or the doorpost; and his master shall bore
> his ear through with an awl; and he shall serve him for life.
>
> 7 "When a man sells his daughter as a slave, she shall not go out as the male
> slaves do.

One can readily notice the moral foundation upon which European and European-American enslavement of the African People was based are these Biblical "ORDINANCES;" and that they are still the basis upon which African-Americans and other peoples of African origin are dealt with to this present day. When we add this to the racist provisions inserted by the Sixth Century Semitic-European rabbis and Talmudists comments about Noah and his sons, as I have shown on page 17 of this Volume, there could be no doubt that Jewish mythological writings have been most responsible for much of the African people's suppression to date.

Let us not forget that up to this period in the biblical writings of the "...INSPIRED SCRIBES..." there is NOTHING suggestive of a "RACE OF PEOPLE" called "HEBREWS, ISRAELITES" or "SEMITES" anywhere in the world; the "WORLD OF GENESIS" or the "WORLD OF EXODUS" as shown on page 35 of this Volume. Again, except for EXODUS, Chapter ii, Verses 1 - 10, which I have extracted and shown below on this page, there is no identification of Moses, or any of the other Hebrews of this period in Africa, that is different to any other indigenous African [BLACK MAN] of Egypt and other Nile Valley High-Cultures; and no other could be justifiably created by "modern" theologians to suit their own "WHITE" racist "negrophobia" and/or "SEMITIC" religious bigotry. Thus we read:

> 1 [Birth and Adoption of Moses] Now a certain man of the house of Levi
> married a Livite woman, 2 who conceived and bore a son. Seeing that
> he was a goodly child, she hid him for three months. 3 When she could
> hide him no longer, she took a papyrus basket, daubed it with bitumen
> and pitch, and putting the child in it, placed it among the reeds on the
> river bank. 4 His sister stationed herself at a distance to find out what
> would happen to him.
>
> 4 Pharaoh's daughter came down to the river to bathe, while her maids
> walked along the river bank, Noticing the basket among the reeds, she
> sent her handmaid to fetch it. 6 On opening it, she looked, and lo, there
> was a baby boy, crying! She was moved with pity for him and said, "It
> is one of the Hebrews' children." 7 Then his sister asked Pharaoh's
> daughter, "Shall I go and call one of the Hebrew women to nurse the child
> for you?" "Yes, do so," she answered. 8 So the maiden went and called
> the child's own mother. 9 Pharaoh's daughter said to her, "Take this child
> and nurse it for me, and I will repay you." 10 The woman therefore took
> the child and nursed it. When the child grew, she brought him to Pharaoh's
> daughter, who adopted him as her son and called him Moses; for she said,
> "I drew him out of the water."

In view of the previous citations in GENESIS and EXODUS; what have we observed so far with respect to the drama of the apparent 'civil strife' between Moses and one group of Africans who worshiped the God YWH against "Pharaoh"[1] Rameses II and another group of Africans who worshiped the God RA?...

> [a] That the continent of Alkebu-lan [Africa] and African people were the focal considerations of the EXODUS story, equally the continent of Asia and Asian people...
>
> [b] it was a story by certain Hebrew [Israelite or Jewish] writers who called each others "...inspired scribes..." in all of their historical recordings which they attributed to their God's [Jehovah or Ywh] guidance; the same God that "created" their own little "world" that extended around the banks of the

---

1. Let us not forget that the word "PHARAOH" is not the name of a "King," as used in the bible; it is instead the title of a "KING." This is one of the fallacies of the entire story.

Tigris and Euphrates River to a distance somewhat beyond the Eastern limits of the Mediterranean Sea [see maps on page 35 of this Volume]; also

[c] the writers account of the famine, which their ancestors found too hard to withstand, caused them to enter Alkebu-lan to seek refuge and haven among the so-called "Negroes", which was carefully underplayed - thus the type of reporting of a "...cruel [African or Negro] Pharaoh..." to redeem their image of being unable to govern their own well-being, which also served to protect their ancestors honor of not being the inferiors to their former hosts in Alkebu-lan [Africa] - the "Negroes;"

[d] the starving, ragged and generally impoverished Asian Hebrews[1] that entered Alkebu-lan returned to their Asian desert well fed, properly clothed and free of the deceases they brought into Alkebu-lan; and following all of this they had engaged in the same type of slave trading of their own people which they complained about when they were enslaved by the worshipers of God RA on their way back to their desert; also out of the clear blue sky a "...certain Pharaoh..." had suddenly came to persecute the same people his great-great grandparents had aided in every manner possible, even to the point of making slaves out of them; and that...

[e] Moses was born of parents who were themselves slaves of African ["Negro" or Black] people; both of said parents being, at best, African-Asian in origin; not Europeans of a "Caucasian" or "Semitic" race; also, that Moses was saved by an African princess who gave him his name - "FETCH FROM WATER," all of which she did in disobedience of her father's LAW AND ORDER against each and every Hebrew "...male child...."

There are many other points we need to examine very closely in order to draw an honest conclusion of who was "RIGHT" or "WRONG" among the people involved in this alleged "EXODUS" drama, since we only have the Hebrews' VERSION of what took place between Moses and his followers and Rameses and his followers. Thus: What caused this "Pharaoh" [Rameses II, ca. 1298 - 1232 B.C.E.] to have suddenly "...enslaved the Israelite people...?" What was the "Pharaoh's" name? What period in African-Asian history and EXPERIENCE did EXODUS happened? Why is there no account of this major event in any of the pharaohs of Egypt metaculous historical recordings of their dynastic reign ? Why did the Hebrews "...inspired writers of Ywh..." ended their "PATRIARCHIAL AGE" with "...Joseph in slavery?" Why did they have to destroy the good image of the African people that saved them from starvation in their own Asian desert before they could have multiplied into the thousands upon thousands they were when they finally left Egypt, Meroe [Sudan] and other High-Cultures of North-east Alkebu-lan?

All of these questions can be answered in the story of "GILGAMESH" - the celebrated

1. The name "ISRAELITES" at this period in history is a grave error. There was no state or High-Culture called "ISRAEL" before the Hebrews entered Africa with Abraham or Jacob et al.

Mesopotanian hero mentioned by a Greek writer named Aelian. But the difference between the story of Moses and that of Gilgamesh is that the "mother" of the latter was the "daughter of the King of Babylon," whose name was Senechores. Also, that she was the one who "became pregnant by an unknown stranger..." while she was still confined to the castle by her wicked father. And following the discovery of her "pregnancy", which was not until one of her father's gardeners found her infant child resting on the ground of a flower garden outside of the castle wall where a passing eagle had lodged it following its rescue of the infant from the fall when she threw it over the parapet. Thus her father's gardner,who found Gilgamesh, became his guardian.[1] Yet the other major point of corelation in this story, as in the story of Moses, was that little Gilgamesh also grew up to challenge the throne of the evil monarch [or Pharaoh] - his own grandfather. Another Greek legend, that of "...the story of Aegisthus - the murderer of Agamemmon,"[2] follows the same line "...the miraculous birth of the saviour of his people." Jesus uprising against his fellow "Jews" is equally in the same context as Moses'.

About the subject of the "MIRACULOUS" [magical] FETES performed by Moses, particularly the "MIRACLE" when his "STAFF [magician's wand] TURNED INTO A SERPENT" upon the command of Ywh. Of course we read about the same type of "MIRACLE" having been performed all over the ancient world of Africa and Asia before the birth of the Hebrew patriarch - Abraham in about ca. 1675 - 1640 B.C.E., muchless before the birth of Moses in Alkebu-lan during ca. 1330 B.C.E.[3] Thus we also read of "...a witch expelling the king's illness..." by touching him with a "...magic wand..." according to the Canaanite "EPIC OF KERET;[4] and of "CIRCE CHANGING ODYSEUS' FRIENDS AND COMPANIONS INTO SWINES" by a touch of the "MAGICIAN'S WAND." As for the case of "MOSES' STAFF" or "ROD" making "THE WATERS OF THE RED SEA PART," the Gods of the African nations along the Great Lakes region of Central Africa were already doing the same; thus one of the Kenda peoples' [nefariously called "Khaffirs"] king[5] -

> "...caused the waters of Lake Tanganyika to part when he raised his staff and purposefully dropped it on the ground...."

1. See T. H. Gaster, THE OLDEST STORIES IN THE WORLD; Sir G. Higgins, ANACALYPSIS, vols. I and II; H. Spaarnay, "Verschmelzung legendarischer und weltliche Motive in der Poesie des Mittelalters, p. 33.
2. Diodorus, SICULUS, ii, p. 4.
3. See I. Abrahams papers, which he read before the Jews' College Literary Society, London 1887, on "Magical Wands;" R. Lenkestester, "DIVERSIONS OF A NATURALIST," [1915], 383-395; Gundel, in P.W.S.V. Rhabdomanteia; E. James, in ERE., s.v. staff.
4. Also known as the "UGARITIC EPIC OF KERET."
5. G. M. Theal, KHAFFIR FOLK-LORE, p. 129.

The story goes on to show that when the King and his own soldiers crossed the "WATERS" of Lake Tanganyika, he once more dropped his "...magical wand..." and:

"...the waters came together and drowned all of the enemies...."

You will notice that I have carefully avoided giving Egyptian, Nubian and Ethiopian corelaries of other EXODUS stories, all in order to show that this type of allegories were, and are, common among the African people from the beginning of the Nile in Central Alkebu-lan down to its ending in Egypt at the Northeastern tip of the continent on the shores of the Mediterranean EXODUS of the Hebrews was just another version of what they had learnt from the Africans with whom the lived in Egypt, Sudan and Meroë - these being the present names of Ta-Merry, Ta-Nehisi and Meröwe [Itiopi], etc. Also, that this type of story is common in Africa to this day wherever the people depend totally for living on a major body of land-lock "WATERS." In other words; it is surely nothing more than a people's FOLK-LORE. I am equally certain that we can observe that Ywh's intervention into the Hebrews mystique, with regards to their own EXODUS story, made it no better, or no worse, than that of other Volume, people's God intercession in their allegorical EXODUS from their own slave masters.

Looking back at the theory of "CREATION" in the Mysteries System's teachings, which was written thousands of years before the other theories mentioned so far in this Volume, we also find that the Africans along the banks of the Blue and White Nile, the Atbara River and the Great Lakes included, as shown in Chapter CXXV of the BOOK OF THE COMING FORTH BY DAY AND BY NIGHT,[1] were required to read the NEGATIVE CONFESSION - of which I have included 29 of the total 147 for your edification on the following page of this Volume; all of which had to be recited in the HALL OF MAATI, including the invocation of the names of many of the "GODS" in order to recapture "LIFE AFTER DEATH" [resurrection or reincarnation]. Some of these GODS I have shown on the front cover design of this work, also on the rear cover. Many of the recitations from the NEGATIVE CONFESSION are common in the papyri dealing with the PYRAMID TEXT, COFFIN TEXT and OSIRIAN DRAMA - all of them having been plagiarized by Moses and/or other Hebrews to form what is today called "THE TEN COMMANDMENTS," and others, in the "FIVE BOOKS OF MOSES [Holy Torah or Old Testament]. And Moses had to know everyone of the NEGATIVE COMMANDMENTS when he received his education in the Mysteries System Lodges [schools, colleges or universities], which was centered at the Grand Lodge of Luxor [Thebes]. You will notice that the indigenous Africans even considered that there were different types of MURDER , STEALING , ROBBERY, etc.; and this included Moses' MURDER OF "THE PHARAOH'S SOLDIER."

1. Budge's English translation is called "EGYPTIAN BOOK OF THE DEAD."

Thus, we noticed that the ancient Africans of the Nile and Great Lakes areas understood that:

"...THERE ARE CIRCUMSTANCES THAT MODERATE WRONG DOINGS...."

Also, that:

"...THE PENALTY FOR CERTAIN WRONGS MUST BE TEMPERED...."

Shall we say that the latter came to us by so-called "MODERN" or "WESTERN LAW?" Equally, that it originated in the British "Magna Carter" [Charter] as an "ACT OF EQUITY?"

EXTRACTS FROM THE "NEGATIVE CONFESSION

[1] I have not done iniquity.
[2] I have not committed robbery with violence.
[3] I have not done violence to no man.
[4] I have not committed theft.
[5] I have not slain man or woman.
[6] I have not made light the bushel.
[7] I have not acted deceitfully.
[8] I have not purloined the things which belonged to the God.
[9] I have not uttered falsehood.
[10] I have not carried away food.
[11] I have not uttered evil words.
[12] I have not attacked man.
[13] I have not killed the beasts which are the property of the Gods.
[14] I have not eaten my heart...i.e., done anything to my regret.
[15] I have not laid waste ploughed land.
[16] I have not pried into matters.
[17] I have not set my mouth against any man.
[18] I have not given way to anger concerning myself without cause.
[19] I have not defiled the wife of a man.
[20] I have not committed transgression against any party.
[21] I have not violated sacred times and seasons.
[22] I have not struck fear into any man.
[23] I have not been a man of anger.
[24] I have not made myself deaf to words of right and truth.
[25] I have not stirred up strife.
[26] I have not made no man weep.
[27] I have not committed acts of impurity or sodomy.
[28] I have not eaten my heart.
[29] I have not abused no man.

At the end of the entire 147 NEGATIVE CONFESSION and the MAGICAL INCANTATION the following instruction appeared:[1]

"This chapter shall be said by the deceased after he hath been cleansed and purified, and when he is arrayed in apparel, and is shod with white leather sandals, and his eyes have been painted with antimony, and his body hath been anointed with anti unguent, and when he hath made offerings of oxen, and birds,

1. Sir E.A.W. Budge's EGYPTIAN MAGIC, pp. 108 - 109; also BOOK OF THE DEAD, Chapter CXXXV.

and incense, and cakes, and ale, and garden herbs. And behold, thou shalt paint a picture of what shall happen in the Hall Of Maati upon a new tile moulded from earth, upon which neither a pig nor any other animal hath trodden. And if thou writest upon it this chapter the deceased shall flourish; and his children shall flourish; and his name shall never fall into oblivion; and bread, and cakes, and sweatmeats, and wine, and meat shall be given unto him at the altar of the great God; and he shall not be turned back at any door in the underworld; and he shall be brought in along with the Kings of the North and South; and he shall be in the following of Osiris always and for ever."

As we have noticed in the vignettes related to the magical works I have just read to you, the pictures of same - with their dramatic coloring in the papyri of the text are profoundly important, each picture and its color amounting to a specific meaning.

Let us not forget that Moses and all of the Hebrews that received their first glimpse into "...civilized education..." in Africa, all of whom lived in the nations of the Nile Valley High-Cultures from ca. 1640 to ca. 1232 B.C.E. - as there were no others elsewhere at this period, passed through the same magical teachings of the Mysteries System as all of the other Nile Valley Africans. And that all of the "MAGIC," or "MIRACLES," Moses performed with his own "STAFF" or "ROD" [magician's wand], even to the "CASTING OF SPELLS,"[2] were already detailed by his African predecessors mentioned in the PYRAMID TEXT, OSIRIAN DRAMA, BOOK OF THE COMING FORTH BY DAY AND BY NIGHT, and PAPYRUS OF ANI,...etc. Even his contemporary "magicians" of Ta-Merry knew they were not "MIRACLES." Thus we find in ACTS, Chapter vii, Verse 22, according to Stephen [later made Saint], the following about Moses:

> He was learned in all the wisdom of the Egyptians,
> and he was mighty in words and deeds...,"etc.

But do we need Stephen to tell us that Moses' "WISDOM" came from the education he received in the Mysteries System's teachings that later on reached all the way into Rome, Greece, Persia and India, among many other lands?[3] Certainly not! Then it should not surprise any of us that Pharaoh Nectabnebus of the XXXth Dynasty [ca. 378 - 360 B.C.E.] and a sage named Aba-aner did all of the MAGIC ["miracles"] Moses performed with their own "STAFF" or "ROD" more than 800 years after Moses and his brother - Aaron - did the same tricks. Thus we see Aaron [in the Old Testament, acting upon the command of his brother Moses] lifting up his "STAFF" and "SMITING THE WATERS" [until it]"TURNED INTO BLOOD...."

---

1. EXODUS vii : 10; also II TIMOTHY iii : 8.
2. Moses "Rod" or "Serpent" swallowed-up the "Rods" or "Serpents" of his fellow Egyptian magicians. The scribes writing this story began with a bias, and so ended with their own fellow religious contemporary as their hero; the losers were bound to be the worshipers of Ra. See also Chabas, "Amales du Musee Guimet," tom. i., pp. 34 - 88, Paris, 1880.
3. See footnote No. 3, p. 5 of this Volume.

And when he stretched the same "STAFF" horizontally over the same "WATERS" thousands of "FROGS APPEARED;" even "...DUST TURNED INTO LICE..." etc., etc., etc.

We are now faced with the major question of this entire Volume. That is; why is it that Moses and Aaron's mysterious magical acts, or fetes [miracles], are to be considered "FACTS" and/or "TRUTHS;" but not those performed before the birth of both, during their lifetime, and following their death, by fellow Africans who worshiped other GODS than Ywh? Because the Hebrew writers of this story, and all of the others involved throughout the entire Old Testament [Holy Torah or Five Books Of Moses], are the self-proclaimed "INSPIRED SCRIBES" we have been brainwashed into believing wrote from some sort of a "MIRACULOUS GIFT FROM GOD - THE ONE AND ONLY" - we have been taught to recognize as a result of biblical RACISM and RELIGIOUS BIGOTRY in our Judaeo-Christian-Islamic education here in the United States of America, Europe, colonial Asia and Africa, and wherever else Judaism, Christianity and/or Islam dominates. Thus we have extended this hostility against all of the peoples in the OLD TESTAMENT who did not allow the Hebrews to do whatever they wanted; and we have equally declared them "ENEMIES" - just like the so-called "Chosen People's... inspired scribes..." who only wrote "...the holy words of God..." had already done. We even condone the wanton acts of GENOCIDE committed by the Hebrews when they exterminated the Hittites, Amalakites, Zebusites, and other weak national groups, in their vicious campaign establishing their own nation; all of this under the excuse that:

> "GOD [Ywh, if one is Jewish; Jesus Christ, if one is Christian; or Al'lah, if one is Moslem] COMMANDED IT TO BE THAT WAY."

I think that if we re-examine the greatest Magical Fete ["MIRACLE"] allegedly performed by Moses according to EXODUS, Chapter xiv, Verses 21 - 28, where it is written:

> 21 Then Moses stretched out his hand over the sea, and the Lord swept the sea
> with a strong east wind throughout the night and so turned it into dry land. When
> the water was thus divided, 22 the Israelites marched into the midst of the sea on
> dry land, with the water like a wall to their right and to their left.
>
> 23 [Destruction of the Egyptians] The Egyptians followed in pursuit; all Pharaoh's
> horses and chariots and charoteers went after them right into the midst of the sea.
> 24 In the night watch just before dawn in the Lord cast through the column to the
> fiery cloud upon the Egyptian force a glance that threw it into a panic; 25 and he so
> clogged their chariot wheels that they could hardly drive. With that the Egyptians
> sounded the retreat before Israel, because the Lord was fighting for them against
> the Egyptians.
>
> 26 Then the Lord told Moses, "Stretch out your hand over the sea, that the water
> may flow back upon the Egyptians, upon their chariots and charioteers." So Moses
> stretched out his hand over the sea, and at dawn the sea flowed back to its normal
> depth. The Egyptians were fleeing head on toward the sea, when the Lord hurled
> them into its midst. As the water flowed back, it covered the chariots and chario-
> teers of Pharaoh's whole army which had followed the Israelites into the sea...,

we have to observe that something radically wrong is taking place, or missing; that is providing we are rational enough to understand that the God of Egypt - RA - had already "COMMANDED" another African of Egypt to "...PART THE WATERS OF THE REED SEA..." long before the God of Moses - "YWH...COMMANDED" him to do likewise later. This we noted in the so-called "WESTCAR PAPYRUS," which professor Erman detailed extensively in his work - "Die Marchen des Papyrus Westcar," Berlin, 1890. And it is equally noted that the "Westcar Papyrus" was written during the XVIIIth Dynasty, sometime between ca. 1555 and 1340 B.C.E. Yet its stories indicate a very much earlier GENESIS, at least during the early dynastic period before ca. 2500 B.C.E., which was also known as "THE PERIOD OF THE EARLY EMPIRE." It even suggests an authorship of the period around the building of one of the "GREAT PYRAMIDS." These facts are evident in the "Westcar Papyrus" itself, for the writings address themselves to matters relative to Pharaoh Khufu[1] and his father, the author being Baui-f-Ra...who also claimed to have "...POSSESSED THE MAGICAL POWER COMMANDED BY KHER HEB [Chief Priest] TCHATCHA-EM-AÑKH...."[2] Thus, we find Pharaoh Khufu saying to Chief Priest Tchatcha-em-añkh:

> "O Tchatcha-em-añkh, my brother, I have done according to thy words, and the heart of my Majesty became glad when I saw how the maidens rowed. But now, an ornament which is made of new turquoise and belongeth to one of the maidens who row hath fallen into the water, and she hath in consequence become silent, and hath ceased to row, and hath disturbed the rowing of those in her company. I said to her, 'Why dost thou not row?' and she replied, 'An ornament [of mine] made of new turquoise hath fallen into the water.' Then I said to her, 'I will get it back for thee.' "

Note that the magical [or "miraculous"] power Tchatcha-em-añkh had, not unlike that attributed to Moses, was given by his God - RA - during the IVth Dynasty [ca. 2670 or 2675 B.C.E.]; and that this gift was given Tchatcha-em-añkh more than 1,300 years before the birth of Moses - who allegedly turned the same trick later on...

> "DIVIDED THE WATERS OF THE REED SEA..."[3] [on the command of the magical words given by another God, Ywh, during the reign of Pharaoh Rameses IInd, XVIII Dynasty, ca. 1298 - 1232 B.C.E.].[4]

The parallels of the magical doings of Moses, exactly following the same fetes of Chief Priest Tchatcha-em-añkh, make one wonder if Moses, like King Solomon and his plagiarization of

---

1. "CHEOPS" or "KHEOPS," according to Herodotus' THE HISTORIES" written in ca. 450 BCE.
2. The Chief Priest in-charge of the priests who conducted the funeral ceremonies from the written magical incantations and teachings of the Mysteries System.
3. See direction of the "REED SEA" on the map on page 54 of this Volume.
4. Words in brackets inserted for the sake of clarity only.

Scribe Amen-em-eope's work - the so-called "PROVERBS OF KING SOLOMON," actually did them ? Strangely enough the ancient Greeks later on called such good works " AMAZING MAGIC;" but today their successors from all over Europe and European-America [the "Western World"] prefer to call them "BLACK MAGIC." Thus, in view of the need for corraborating evidence, I have provided you with a few examples of the comparisons between the so-called "PROVERBS OF KING SOLOMON" and "THE TEACHINGS OF AMEN-EM-EOPE" to see how the latter's work was plagiarized to produce the former's VERSION...

THE COMPARATIVE WORKS

The Teachings Of Amen-em-eope Egypt [Northeast Alkebu-lan]	Proverbs xxii : 17, xxiii : 14 Israel [Asia Minor]
1. Give thine ear, and hear what I say, And apply thine heart to apprehend; It is good for thee to place them in thine heart, Let them rest in the casket of thy belly. That they may act as a peg upon thy tongue.	1a. Incline thine ear, and hear my words, And apply thine heart to apprehend; For it is pleasant if thou keep them in thy belly, That they may be fixed like a peg upon they lips.
2. Consider these thirty chapters; They delight, they instruct. Knowledge how to answer him that speaketh, And how to carry back a report to one that sent him	2a. Have I not written for thee thirty sayings. Of consels and knowledge! That thou mayest make known truth to him that speaketh.
3. Beware of robbing the poor, And of oppressing the afflicted.	3a. Rob not the poor for he is poor, Neither oppress the lowly in the gate.

For further details of "THE COMPARATIVE WORKS" I have just read to you see AFRICAN ORIGINS OF THE MAJOR "WESTERN RELIGIONS," pages 71 and 72.

In the Second Book of the METAMORPHOSE OF APULEUIS the student named "Telephron," while in a place called "LARISSA" and penniless, hungry,and without lodging, inquired of an elderly man about the strange custom of the indigenous people in regards to their "...guarding of the dead...," etc. He asked:

" WILL THE DEAD FLEE THE CITY IF THEY ARE NOT GUARDED BY THE LIVING?"

1. See Sir E. A. Wallis Budge's, EGYPTIAN MAGIC, p. 11.

One of his hosts quickly enlightened him on the fact that:

> "...the witches of Thessaly used to snatch hunks of the faces of the dead with their pointed fang-like teeth and feed them to their demons for the purpose of making magic for evil spells...."

This dialogue continued, almost endlessly; but at one point it dealt with a woman who had killed her nephew to gain his wealth so that she could have gotten married. And that following this she was being stoned, at which time she was overheard beseeching her GODS to witness her "...innocense...," etc.... to which one of her accusers hollered in rebuttal - according to E.A. Wallis Budge's EGYPTIAN MAGIC, pages 13 and 14:

> "...in the underworld, and to make it to dwell in his body again for a short time. With these words, he Let, them, Divine Providence decide the truth, in answer to her denial. Behold, the famous prophet, Zaclas the Egyptian, dwelleth among us, and he hath promised me that for much money he will make the soul of the dead man to return from the place of death...," etc.

Here, again, we have seen that the indigenous Africans of Egypt, as other Nile Valley High-Cultures could...

> "MAKE THE SOUL OF THE DEAD MAN... RETURN FROM THE PLACE OF DEATH IN THE UNDERWORLD[1]..." [etc., and] "...COULD MAKE IT DWELL IN HIS BODY AGAIN FOR A SHORT TIME...," [etc.].

The last two quotations should remind all of us that the biblical Moses did nothing strange, or new, with all of the "MIRACLES" [magic] attributed to him by his fellow Hebrews. Even Jesus Christ of Nazareth's raising of "...LAZARUS FROM THE DEAD...," according to JOHN, Chapter ii, Verses 1 - 44 of the Christian NEW TESTAMENT [Holy Bible, irrespective of versions], did nothing new with "HIS MIRACULOUS POWER." Professor George G.M. James made this point very clear when he noted the following about Moses and Jesus Christ, with respect to their training in "MAGIC" at the Mysteries System's Grand Lodge [college or university] on page 178 of his major work - STOLEN LEGACY. He wrote:

> [6] All the great religious leaders from Moses to Christ were Initiates of the Egyptian Mysteries.
>
> This is an inference from the nature of the Egyptian Mysteries and prevailing custom.
>
> [a] The Egyptian Mystery System was the One Holy Catholic Religion of the remotest antiquity.
>
> [b] It was the one and only Masonic Order of Antiquity, and as such,
>
> [c] It built the Grand Lodge of Luxor in Egypt and encompassed the ancient world with its branch lodges.
>
> [d] It was the first University of history and it made knowledge secret,

---

1. Where the deceased pharaoh was placed to begin his journey in the "NETHERWORLD" - the Tomb or Pyramid. This is equivalent to the Christian's "HEAVEN."
2. See JOHN xi : 1 - 44

so that all who desired to become Priests and Teachers had to obtain their training from the Mystery System, either locally at a branch lodge or by traveling to Egypt.

We know that Moses became an Egyptian Priest, a Hierogrammat, and that Christ after attending the lodge at Mt. Carmel went to Egypt for Final Initiation, which took place in the Great Pyramid of Cheops. Other religious leaders obtained their preparation from lodges most convenient to them.

[e] This explains why as religions, seemingly different, have a common nucleus of similarity; belief in a God; belief in immorality and a code of ethics. Read Ancient Mysteries by C.H. Vail, p. 61; Mystical Life of Jesus by H. Spencer Lewis; Esotoric Christianity by Annie Besant, p. 107, 128 - 129; Philo; also read note [2] Chapter III for branch lodges of the ancient world.

Moses, a native of Egypt,[1] was like all of the other indigenous Africans of Egypt and other parts of Alkebu-lan [Africa] in terms of "COLOR." Even the nation in Alkebu-lan where he was born was given the name "KAMT" as a result of the "COLOR" of the people therein - "BLACK" [the English translation of the Egyptian word - "Kamt" or "Qemt"]. However; I must advise you of the cutest explanation of this name, so far as your instructor have been able to find in my most exhaustive investigation to date, is one detailed by the English "egyp - tologist" of note Sir Ernest A. Wallis Budge in his book - EGYPTIAN MAGIC, pages 19 and 20, which I have extracted and shown below on this page. Budge wrote:

> One of the oldest names of Egypt is "Kamt" or Qemt," a word which means "black" or "dusky," and it was applied to the country on account of the dark colour of the mud which forms the land on each side of the Nile; the Christian Egyptian or Copts transmitted the word under the form Khême to the Greeks, Romans, Syrians, and Arabs.

However, is it not strange that the so-called "father of [European and European-American] history," Herodotus, sometime between ca. 450 to 447 B.C.E. should have described the indigenous people of Egypt ["Kamt"] in the following manner...in light of Budge's conclusion? Herodotus wrote:[2]

> "The Colchians, Egyptians and Ethiopians have thick lips, broad nose, woolly hair, and they are burnt of skin...."

I guess people like Budge and the Judaeo-Christian-Islamic theologians of the 19th Century C.E., equally those of the 20th Century C.E., would have preferred to maintain their lily-white "Semitic" and "Hamitic" OLD TESTAMENT, NEW TESTAMENT and HOLY QURAN; and would also like us to accept that the Egyptians [Romiti] and other ancient Nile Valley Africans

---

1. Also called "Kimit, Kamt, Qemt, Ta-Merry," etc. before the present name given to this land by Hebrew writers in their mythology about the grandsons of Noah.
2. See Herodotus' THE HISTORIES [as translated by Wilson Armisted in London, 1848], p. 12

received their "...BURNT [black] SKIN..." from Budge's "...DARK COLOUR OF THE MUD WHICH FORMS THE LAND ON EACH SIDE OF THE NILE...." And of course; should African people not finally call upon enough of their courageous scholars to do what all of the other so-called "ETHNIC [white] GROUPS" [European-American Jews, and European-American Christians - Mormons, Jehovah Witnesses, Christian Scientists, Quakers, etc.] have done to their own Judaeo-Christian theology? Obviously, the question in your mind is; What have they done? The answer is; they have...

> REVISED GENESIS AND ALL OF THE OTHER BOOKS OF THE OLD AND NEW TESTAMENT TO SUIT THEIR OWN ETHNIC NEEDS AND RELIGIOUS BIGOTRY; REMOVED AND SUPPRESSED OTHERS UNDER THE PRETENSE OF THEIR BEING "LOST BOOKS OF THE BIBLE," ETC., ETC., ETC.

But let me remind each and everyone of you that the so-called "LOST BOOKS OF THE BIBLE" you had in your hand a few weeks ago in the library at my house is still available for purchase at the World Publishing Company; and that the "BOOKS" that were allegedly "LOST" were in fact removed at the so-called "COUNCIL OF BISHOPS" at Nycene [or Nicene] upon the ORDER or "EDICT" of Emperor Constantine "the great" in the year 325 C.E.

Now that we will have to paint all of the Nile Valley indigenous Africans "MUD," or at least "COLOURED," whatever these two terms mean, it is obvious that the Africans of GENESIS and EXODUS did not have the luxury of this type of racist emotion that engulfs each and every institution of "Western Civilization" [society]; at least not against their own color; but we will equally have to paint them, and those who wrote the BOOK OF THE COMING FORTH BY DAY AND BY NIGHT, PAPYRUS OF ANI, COFFIN TEXT, PYRAMID TEXT, OSIRIAN DRAMA, NEGATIVE CONFESSION, etc. in "MUD" and/or "COLOURED" like their "modern" BLACK brothers I have shown on pages 56 through 60 of this Volume. I have given detailed information about all of them in BLACK MAN OF THE NILE AND HIS FAMILY, AFRICA: MOTHER OF "WESTERN CIVILIZATION," AFRICAN ORIGIN OF THE MAJOR "WESTERN RELIGIONS," CULTURAL GENOCIDE IN THE BLACK AND AFRICAN STUDIES CURRICULUM, also in some of my other works you have already examined.

It is needless to mention that the geography of the land over which the EXODUS of more than 400,000 Hebrew people from one part of Egypt - SUCCOTH...to another part of the same nation - the SINAI PENINSULA...could not have been the place mentioned in the Bible, unless all of the people that crossed it equally suffered a major catastrophy. And that nobody all over the other High-Cultures of the entire more than 4,100 miles long Nile River [from Uganda in Central East Africa to the Mediterranean Sea at the shores of North Africa] knew about it. Because of this impossibility I have included an enlarged map of the "ROUTE OF THE EXODUS" and the geo-political entities that existed during said period of the African-Asian experience demonstrated in the graphic presentation on the map on this page.

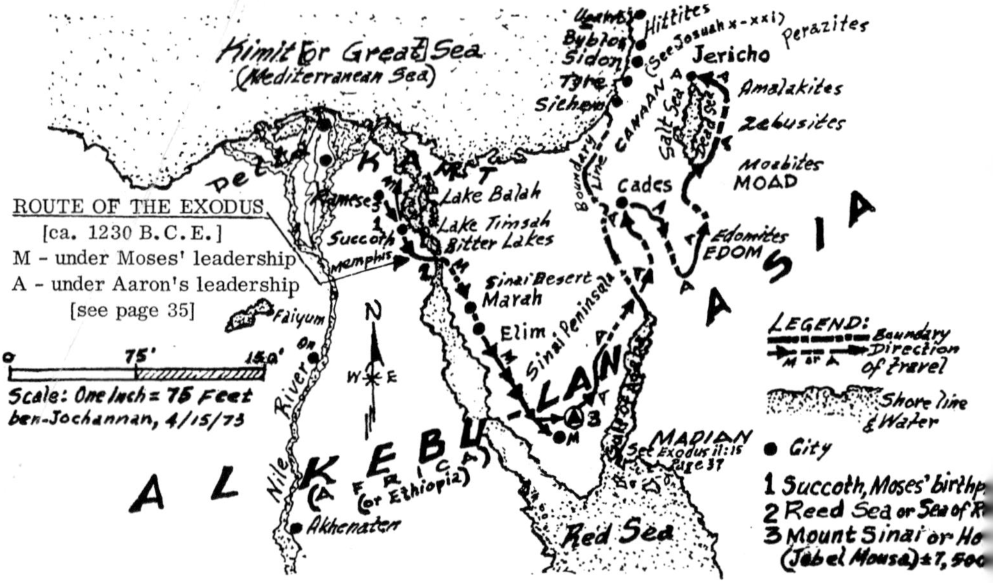

Having examined the so-called "ROUTE OF THE EXODUS" the Hebrews took in their dri to establish their own nation they later called "ISRAEL," it is obvious that there should hav been other records of this allegedly "...GREATEST OF ALL EVENTS IN NILE VALLEY HISTORY..." written by the 'GOD INSPIRED [indigenous African] SCRIBES' of Ta-Nehisi, Itiopi, Meroë, and of course Kamt - where the EXODUS allegedly had its genesis. But woul it have been possible for the "SACRED SCRIBES" of Punt,[1] Lebus,[2] Numidia[3] and Khart-Had not to have heard about the EXODUS from relatives, travellers and students, or at least fro their ambassadors and other dignitaries assigned to the various High-Cultures [nations] alon the banks of the Nile Valley [blue and white], Atbara River and Great Lakes regions, equally in Punt at the furthest point where the Red Sea meets the Indus Ocean? For we know that the was always contact with the indigenous Africans all the way from Kamt to Punt; this we can still read about in Queen Hatshep-sut's voyage to her relatives in Punt; the same as we have read about other monarchs of Kamt who made it their "SACRED DUTY" to visit the "LAND

1. A nation of Northeast Alkebu-lan that occupied most of present-day Somalia, parts of Ken and Tanganyika, and much of colonial "French Somaliland" [renamed "Afar" etc.].
2. Presently most of what is today called "Libya" and part of "Tunisia."
3. The birthplace of St. Augustine; generally part of what is today "Algeria" and "Tunisia."
4. The so-called "Carthaginian Empire;" parts of Morocco and Algeria today.

FROM WHENCE CAME THE GODS" - Punt, the "LAND WHERE THE GODS LOVE TO BE" - Ethiopia, and the "...LAND OF THE MOUNTAIN OF THE MOON..." [Kenya and Uganda, where Kilamanjaro - "Mountain Of The Moon" stands in her majesty] at the beginning of the Nile River. Queen Hatshep-sut's voyage to Punt was made during her own reign over Egypt and many other lands her father Thotmosis I left her at the end of his reign - ca. 1515 B.C.E, her reign having lasted from ca. 1515 to1484 B.C.E. I have shown the report of her entire voyage in HIEROGLYPH on page 57 of this Volume . Note that there were voyages in the opposite directions by monarchs from Punt, Meröe, Itiopi and Ta-Nehisi to their relatives and fellow monarchs of Kamt, as I have shown on page 60. The top scene shows a very old and deformed Queen of Punt upon her arrival in Kamt on an "OFFICIAL STATE VISIT." The bottom scene shows the Ta-Nehisian relatives of Pharaoh Tut-ankh-Amen taking gifts to him during the XVIIIth Dynasty, ca. ? - 1349 B.C.E., all of whom were equally on an "OFFICIAL STATE VISIT." But is it not strange that most of your professors and teachers have always said that the Africans from south of Kamt came only as "SLAVES" to that empire at the North ?

You will notice that European and European-American "EGYPTOLOGISTS" and "LIBERAL HISTORIANS" of European-American academia had no problem in finding that which show Ta-Nehisians, Itiopians and Puanits as "SLAVES" will not equally make professor Frank W. Snowden's BLACKS IN ANTIQUITY: A GRECO-ROMAN EXPERIENCE, published by Harvard University Press in 1971, one of the required books of a course. Why; you asked? Because it deals with an extensive detailing of African [BLACK] People we have always accepted as being Greeks and Romans of "Caucasian, Semitic, White, European-Aryan stock," some of whom I have shown on page 59 of this Volume , and documented on page 60. You will also note that I have made this fact very clear in CULTURAL GENOCIDE IN THE BLACK AND AFRICAN STUDIES CURRICULUM; BLACK MAN OF THE NILE AND HIS FAMILY; and AFRICA: MOTHER OF "WESTERN CIVILIZATION;" and in all of my other works.

What you have seen unfolded before you in the AFRICAN EXPERIENCE is not an attempt to 'BLACKEN' everything pertaining to the BOOK OF GENESIS and/or the BOOK OF EXODUS, but instead a correction of the accomplished "WHITE-OUT" of the "BLACKS" of these first two of the so-called "FIVE BOOKS OF MOSES," and all of the other three.

As I move into the area of giving my personal CONCLUSION no documentary is needed on the course of what all of this mean to me, not only as a professor of HISTORY and RELIGION, but as a son of "Mother Alkebu-lan" like the millions more in the Harlems of the entire world. I must remind all of you as students of African, African-American, African-European, African-Asian, etc. HISTORY and HERITAGE that the last of the pictures of this Volume on page 60 bears the blunt of this entire socio-political and religious catostrophic attempt of CAUCASIAN-

ISM and SEMITISM that exist in the present VERSIONS of the Holy Torah [Old Testament or Five Books Of Moses], Holy Bible [or New Testament] and Holy Quran [or Koran] about all that was, and still is, ISRAEL.

THE NEW YORK TIMES, FRIDAY, MARCH 4, 1955

Falasha Jews From Ethiopia Studying in Israel [1]

Isazah Adomic, 16-year-old leader of Falasha youngsters studying at Kfar Batya in Israel, serves Malka Avraham. Another Falasha student and an Israeli friend await their turns.

Their ancestry goes back to time of King David [1]

n religious high school, integration is the rule and girls attend classes along with the boys. Compulsory education for all is the rule in Israel.

1. See CULTURAL GENOCIDE IN THE BLACK AND AFRICAN STUDIES CURRICULUM, p. 18

The Only Queen In History Officially Listed As A King

Māt-ka-Rā, son of the Sun, Ḥāt-shepset-χnem-Āmen,

A photographic view (from the north-east) of the ruins of Queen Hatshepsut s Funeary at Luxor [Thebes] or Deir el-Bahri

The splendor of Egypt's architecture is best exhibited in this structure. Modern public buildings fall short of its beauty and colossal magnitude.

HAT-SHEP-SUT, XVIIIth Dynasty, c. 1515 - 1484, the FIRST QUEEN in history to rule over a nation. Limestone statue, Museum of Art.

QUEEN HATSHEPSUT'S EXPEDITION TO THE LAND OF PUNT.[1]

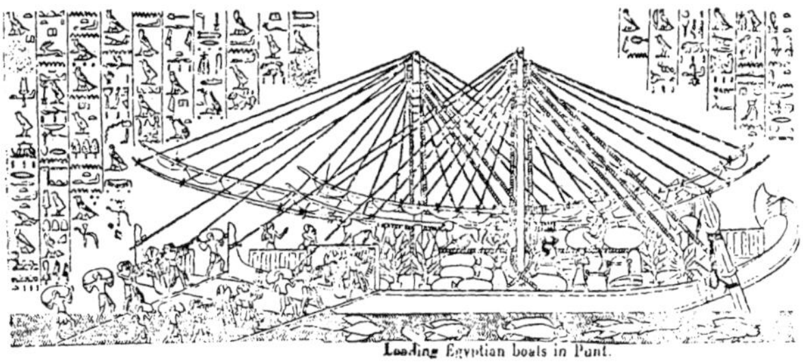

Loading Egyptian boats in Punt.

1. See Y. ben-Jochannan's BLACK MAN OF THE NILE AND HIS FAMILY, p. 284

THE QUEEN OF PUNT (CAIRO MUSEUM)[1]

NUBIANS BRINGING TRIBUTE TO TUTANKHAMUN[2]
(THEBES, TOMB OF HUY)

Ethnic Permanency Impossible. "By migration and conquest the original racial factors, whatever they were, have been so interwoven and blended that the vast majority of all living men must have a complex racial ancestry, and such a thing as a pure race can hardly be expected to live." And again: "There is not a race in all history that has remained permanently unchanged, although the rate and degree of change have varied."[3]

1. See Y. ben-Jochannan's AFRICA: MOTHER OF "WESTERN CIVILIZATION," p. 262.
2. Ibid., p. 263.
3. See Dixon's RACIAL HISTORY OF MAN, Introduction, p. 4. Professor Dixon defines his terms thusly: "From the standpoint of the anthropologist...a race is a biological group, based on community of physical characters." Groups characterized solely on linguistic, cultural or political unity he called a "stock" and/or "nation." - 1. c. p. 3.

Note: For the key to all of the figures above see the top of the following page - 60.

KEY TO PAGE 59 [1]

1. Bronze bust of a "Negro" Roman, from G. Calaza, "Expression of Art in a Roman Commercial City: Ostia," Journal Of Roman Studies V [1915], 165-167, fig. 41.
3. Pharaoh Taharqa from Ethiopia, XXV th Dynasty of Egypt [Ta-Merry].
5. "Negro" Roman ambassador of the Flavian period. [Rome, Villa Albani, 209, Deutsches Archaologisches Instituto, Rome].
7. Pharaoh Amenohat III of Ta-Merry, the so-called "NEGRO PHARAOH."

2. Marble head of "Negro" Roman found at Agora, Trajonic period. ["The Excavation of the Athenian Agora Twelfth Season," by H.A. Thompson, 1947].
4."Negro"Greek of the 4th Century B.C.E.
6. Sphinx Of Ghizeh, Ta-Merry [according tc a painting by Baron Viviant Denon, "Travels In Egypt and Assyria," France, 1895].
8. Pharaoh Aspelta of Ta-Merry.
9. Faience Vace of "Negro" Cypriot, late 7th Century B.C.E., with bearded bar - barian. [British Museum, A7 8-6 2D].

10. Roman Emperor Caracalla, son of Roman Emperor Septimus Severus, Rome, 193 A.D. Both of African origin - father of African birth, Carthage; son of Syrian mother.

African-American Israelites at prayer in Harlem's Commandments Keepers Of Ethiopian Hebrews Congregation, Harlem, New York City, New York.[2]

1. All of the above are of African birth or origin; some with Asian, European, European-American or Caribbean lineage. See F.W. Snowden's BLACKS IN ANTIQUITY: A GRECO-ROMAN EXPERIENCE; J.A. Rogers' WORLD'S GREAT MEN OF COLOR, vol. I; Y. ben-Jochannan's AFRICA MOTHER OF "WESTERN CIVILIZATION; G.G.M. James' STOLEN LEGACY.
2. Today these BLACK ISRAELITES, and hundreds of thousands like them, are the conscience of European and European-American Semitic-Caucasian [WHITE] - dominated and racially oriented Israel - "THE LAND OF THE CANAANITES."

BIBLIOGRAPHY FOR LECTURE No. II

[Books listed according to chronological order of appearance in the text]

OLD TESTAMENT [Confraternity Version, Guild Press, New York, 1961]

H. Fishberg, THE JEWS, London, 1911

Y. ben-Jochannan, BLACK MAN OF THE NILE AND HIS FAMILY, New York, 1972

G.G.M. James, STOLEN LEGACY, New York, 1954

Philo, CLAERON: Jos. C. Apion I

Dr. J. Hastings, BIBLE DICTIONARY, New York, 1890

C.H. Vail, ANCIENT MYSTERIES, New York

T.H. Gaster, THE OLDEST STORIES IN THE WORLD, New York, 1952

Sir G. Higgins, ANACALYPSIS, London, 1848 [2 Vols.]

H. Spaarnay, "Verschnelzung legendarischer und Weltliche Motive in der Poesie des Muttelaters," Germany, 1922

Diodorus, SICULUS

Abrahams Papers on "Magical Wands" [in: JEWS COLLEGE LITERARY SOCIETY, London, 1887]

P. Lenkestester, DIVERSIONS OF A NATURALIST, Berlin, 1915

G. Gundel's P.W.S.V. Rhabdomanteia

E. James' ERE., S.V. STAFF

Homer, ODYSSEY, 10.238

G.M. Theal, KHAFFIR FOLK-LORE, London, 1886

Sir E.A. Wallis Budge, EGYPTIAN BOOK OF THE DEAD, London, 1885

------------ PAPYRUS OF ANI, London, 1885

NEGATIVE CONFESSION [translated into English by Pete]

PYRAMID TEXT

OSIRIAN DRAMA

Sir E. A. Wallis Budge, EGYPTIAN MAGIC, New York, 1889

E. Erman, "Westcar Papyrus" [in: Die Marchen des Papyrus Westcar, Berlin, 1890]

METAMORPHOSE OF APULEUS

Y. ben-Jochannan, AFRICAN ORIGINS OF THE MAJOR "WESTERN RELIGIONS," New York, 1971

A. Besant, ESOTORICAL CHRISTIANITY, New York,

H. Spencer Lewis, MYSTICAL LIFE OF JESUS, New York

Herodotus, THE HISTORIES, Book II [ca. 457 - 450 B.C.; as translated into English by Williams, London, 1884]

W. Armistead, A TRIBUTE TO THE NEGRO, London, 1848

Y. ben-Jochannan, CULTURAL GENOCIDE IN THE BLACK AND AFRICAN STUDIES CURRICULUM, New York, 1973

F.W. Snowden, BLACKS IN ANTIQUITY: A Greco-Roman Experience, Cambridge, Massachusettes, 1971

St. Augustine's CONFESSIONS [as translated into English by Pussey]

------- ------ CITY OF GOD [as translated into English by Pussey]

G. Calaza, 'EXPRESSION OF ART IN A ROMAN COMERCIAL CITY: OSTIA"[in: Journal of Roman Studies, V., 1915]

H. A. Thompson, "The Excavations of the Athenian Agora Twelfth Season," 1973

Baron V. Denon, TRAVELS IN EGYPT AND ASSYRIA, Paris, 1895

J.A. Rogers, WORLD'S GREAT MEN OF COLOR, New York, 1954 [Vol. I]

MY CONCLUSION:
GENESIS and EXODUS A PART OF THE BLACK EXPERIENCE.

Realizing that the entire FIVE BOOKS OF MOSES represent a one-sided report by people who were the 'COMPLAINANTS, WITNESSES, PROSECUTORS, JUDGES, JURORS,' and even the only "CHOSEN PEOPLE OF GOD," all of them on the side of the so-called "ISRAELITES;" if I have not satisfactorily looked at the other side at this juncture, and proved that GENESIS and EXODUS are allegorical, mythological, poetical, historical, geo-political and anthropological stories that are mixed with the religious taboos by ancient men of an African-Asian origin; and if in fact the stories actually happened ; then, there is very little more I could present to you that I would present to other students to make any of them see beyond their rather narrow exclusive Judaeo-Christian-Islamic "TRUTH" that is tied to his or her racial PREJUDICE and/or religious BIGOTRY. But one thing is certain, there were no Europeans on the scene of GENESIS and EXODUS; and not one was mentioned by any of the so-called "SACRED SCRIBES" in any of their "INSPIRED WORDS" they received from their Hebrew or Israelite God - "YWH" [Jehovah or Adoni]. And we know that the closest period to the existence of anything called "WESTERN CIVILIZATION" in terms of years from the Hebrews "EXODUS" from Alkebu-lan was more than ca. 632 years. This "BLACK EXPERIENCE" included the death of Rameses II, the last pharaoh of the XIXth Dynasty, in ca. 1232 B.C.E., the Pharaoh with whom Moses had his personal vandetta ['civil war']. Very much later it even included the period when Greek literacy and literature were first verified - i.e. Homer's publication of his two works - the ILIAD and ODYSSEY - in approximately ca. 600 B.C.E., which was equivalent in time to the XXVIth Dynasty of Egyptian rule under Pharaoh Necho's reign...ca. 609 - 594 B.C.E. All of this took place at the end of the Nile Valley in Africa.

The validity of an African-Asian GENESIS and African-Asian EXODUS does not depend upon this treatise, nor does it upon anyother person's hypothetical work. For if in fact the Judaeo-Christian-Islamic GENESIS and EXODUS were realities, they would have been impossible without their indigenous "AFRICAN [black] PEOPLE'S EXPERIENCE" in Africa and their "ASIAN [brown and yellow] PEOPLE'S EXPERIENCE" in Asia. Thus, one has to understand that the reason for the presentation of my treatise to you, as students, is not to secure your endorsement of the validity of either ratinnale, in so far as their actual occurance, but instead for your analytical appreciation of the amount of research necessary to pinpoint the imput of the RACISM and RELIGIOUS BIGOTRY connected thereto through the efforts of 'ex-post-facto' would be representatives of the God-head called "YWH, JESUS CHRIST" and/or "AL'LAH." For neither of these God-heads ever "WROTE" a single "WORD" anywhere; nor "CURSED" a single person any place other than in one's mind. Thus, I am demonstrating that it is always somebody saying that somebody else...etc., etc., etc..., almost endlessly, said that:

"GOD [Ywh, Jesus Christ, Al'lah, etc.] SAID" [this, and/or that] WHEN," etc.

But the "TRUTH" of the matter lies in one's belief, which is otherwise called "FAITH." But "FAITH" is not necessarily "TRUTH," or even "FICTION."

Why "GOD" could not have had a single NEGRO" [Black, Brown, Yellow, or whatever] involved as one of his many "PROPHETS, DISCIPLES" or "HOLY INSPIRED SCRIBES?" Because He too must have been a "RACIST" and/or "RELIGIOUS BIGOT;" at least this is what I am led to believe, if I am to give the standard depiction of the African and Asian characters of the biblical stories painted by European and European-American artists for their synagogues, temples, churches, mosques, and other houses of religious worship - where constant written propaganda of each RELIGIOUS FAITH is manufactured in the same manner as "throw-aways" for the local, regional and national political elections my consideration as "TRUTH."

Since the CLERGY has become just another job in the world of employment for most, and a "get-rich quick scheme" for many; and since promotion in said "BUSINESS" depends primarily upon internal political maneuvering within religious institutions; it is, or should be, understandable that the CLERGY [Jewish, Christian or Moslem] can be no less "EVIL" in every manner than the society which it perpetuates and protects. The vast majority of the members of the CLERGY as a general rule, I have to remember, are from the same racist or bigoted religious neighbourhoods their parishoners are part of. And since their general socio-political upbringing is the same as all of the others involved in the so-called "BLACK-WHITE CONFRONTATION;" also, since they too are nothing more than mere mortals - including the Grand Rabbi, Pope and Grand Emir; then maybe Ywh, Jesus Christ and/or Al'lah may prove to be "personae non gratis" upon either, or all of them, return to those who constantly call upon either of their names as they commit their acts of RACISM and RELIGIOUS BIGOTRY; this, too, I must remember.

Probably when human beings can have their own GENESIS [birth] without labels of "BASTARD, HALF-BREED, ILLIGITIMATE, LOVE CHILD, OUT OF WEDLOCK BABE," and other such social stigma based upon religious anti-sexual bias from the ADAM AND EVE and "THE FORBIDDEN FRUIT TREE" syndrome attached to them, as they are perpetuated today by those who appointed themselves..."SAVIOURS" of mankind; then shall another day come when the "WORD" of all of the "GODS" will be in "GENESIS" again. And maybe at that time mankind will be able to say without fear of recrimination from Jews, Christians and Moslems, irrespective of our Judaeo-Christian-Islamic theory of a biblical GENESIS...;

' I DO NOT KNOW. '

Only at that time can we TRULY admit that no one, HOLY or UNHOLY, GODLY or UNGODLY, DEVINE BEING or SPIRIT, appointed any of US to "SAVE THE WORLD FROM SIN."

Just imagine how 'GODLY" it will be to be free from the prostylizing missionaries who need to pay heed to their own prophecies they are trying to sell to others who have their own. Then, maybe GOD'S KINGDOM ON EARTH will be free of RACIAL and RELIGIOUS conflict over the following palaeontological, geopolitical and socio-political "TRUTH:"

> MOSES WAS AN AFRICAN; BORN IN AFRICA; BROUGHT UP AND EDUCATED IN AFRICA IN THE RELIGION OF RA; WAS EMPLOYED AS AN OFFICIAL IN THE EGYPTIAN GOVERNMENT; FOUGHT TO FREE AFRICAN HEBREWS IN AFRICA; ESTABLISHED THE BASIC TENETS OF "JUDAISM" FROM THE LAWS AND PHILOSOPHY OF RELIGION HE LEARNT FROM HIS FELLOW AFRICANS IN THE MYSTERIES SYSTEM OF THE GRAND LODGE OF LUXOR ON THE NILE; EXPIRED IN AFRICA, WHERE HE WAS BURIED BEFORE THE COMPLETION OF THE HEBREWS EXODUS OUT OF AFRICA AND INTO ASIA ... ;

all of this providing that "GENESIS" and "EXODUS" are of the "WORD."

"The World" That Produced "Genesis," "Exodus" & "Judaism"

All Faith is FALSE, all FAITH is TRUE
    TRUTH is the shattered mirrors strewn
In myriad bits; while each believes
    his little bit the whole to own.[1]

---

1. From "THE KASIDAH OF Haji Abu el-Yezdi" [as translated by Sir Richard F. Burton].

2. The "WORLD" of the Hebrews did not include any nation they did not know, such as all of the so-called "Western World," most of Asia, Africa, and Europe, and equally the islands.

Before we enter into the sources from whence this work was developed, and also into the text of Volume III - THE NEED FOR A BLACK BIBLE, let yourself be reminded of the fact that even Jesus Christ did not claim to be GOD, as stated in the following extract from Matthew, xvi : 13 - 14:

13 ¶ When Jē'-ṣŭs came into the coasts of Çæ-ṣă-rē'-ă Phi-lip'-pi, he asked his disciples, saying, Whom do men say that I the Son of man am? 14 And they said, Some *say that thou art* Jōhn the Băp'-tist: some, Ē-lī'-ăs; and others, Jĕr-ē-mī'-ăs, or one of the prophets.

The above is from the KING JAMES VERSION; the following is from the REVISED STANDARD VERSION:

13 Now when Jesus came into the district of Caes·a·rē'a Phi·lip'pi, he asked his disciples, "Who do men say that the Son of man is?" 14 And they said, "Some say John the Baptist, others say E·li'jah, and others Jeremiah or one of the prophets." 15

And as we deal with Matthew, very much like we deal with all of the disciples except Paul of Tarsus [formerly Saul of Tarsus], let us not forget that Jesus Christ was described in full details by Jeremiah. For example in Jeremiah, viii : 21 he said the following about his own Hebrew [Jewish] People, the same as Jesus:

21 For the hurt of the daughter of my people am I hurt; I am black; astonishment hath taken hold on me.

The REVISED STANDARD VERSION again differs fundamentally with the KING JAMES VERSION; the latter being shown above; the former appears as follow:

21 For the wound of the daughter of my people is my heart wounded I mourn, and dismay has taken hold on me.

Jeremiah was equally as emphatic about the identity of COLOR when he asked:

"CAN THE ETHIOPIAN CHANGE HIS SKIN, OR THE LEOPARD HIS SPOTS?!"..

in Jeremiah, xiii : 23 as much as he was in xiv : 2, where he stated:

2 Jū'-dăh mourneth, and the gates thereof languish; they are black unto the ground; and the cry of Jĕ-ru'-să-lĕm is gone up,..

according to the KING JAMES VERSION; which the REVISED STANDARD VERSION recorded in the following manner:

2 "Judah mourns and her gates languish; her people lament on the ground, and the cry of Jerusalem goes up.

Citing Jeremiah for the last time, particularly in his woes, which he recorded under the heading of LAMENTATIONS, as in the following extract from v : 1 - 10:

REMEMBER, O LORD, what is come upon us: consider, and behold our reproach.
2 Our inheritance is turned to strangers, our houses to aliens.
3 We are orphans and fatherless, our mothers *are* as widows.
4 We have drunken our water for money; our wood is sold unto us.
5 Our necks *are* under persecution: we labour, *and* have no rest.
6 We have given the hand *to* the E-gyp'-tians, *and to* the As-syr'-i-ans, to be satisfied with bread.
7 Our fathers have sinned, *and are* not; and we have borne their iniquities.
8 Servants have ruled over us: *there is* none that doth deliver *us* out of their hand.
9 We gat our bread with *the peril of* our lives because of the sword of the wilderness.
10 Our skin was black like an oven because of the terrible famine.

The following is the REVISED STANDARD VERSION of the above:

5 Remember, O LORD, what has befallen us;
behold, and see our disgrace!
2 Our inheritance has been turned over to strangers,
our homes to aliens.
3 We have become orphans, fatherless;
our mothers are like widows.
4 We must pay for the water we drink,
the wood we get must be bought.
5 With a yoke[u] on our necks we are hard driven;
we are weary, we are given no rest.
6 We have given the hand to Egypt,
and to Assyria, to get bread enough.
7 Our fathers sinned, and are no more;
and we bear their iniquities.
8 Slaves rule over us;
there is none to deliver us from their hand.
9 We get our bread at the peril of our lives,
because of the sword in the wilderness.
10 Our skin is hot as an oven
with the burning heat of famine.

The above extracts conflict with other VERSIONS [see pages 82 - 86 of Volume III] of the so-called OLD TESTAMENT and NEW TESTAMENT.

The pattern of racism established in both of the above VERSIONS of the so-called OLD TESTAMENT and NEW TESTAMENT will be found in all of the different VERSIONS of every one of the so-called "HOLY SCRIPTURES" of the Jewish, Christian and Judaeo-Christian type religious teachings throughout Europe, Great Britain and the Americas; needless to mention other areas of the world dominated by European and European-American "Christian Missionary" propaganda introduced to the indigenous victims of those lands since the beginning of colonialism and neo-colonialism from Europe and European-America. These distorted views and interpretations of the "HOLY BIBLE" [Old Testament or New Testament] demand that African [BLACK] People all over the world MUST redevelop their own "HOLY BIBLE" as they once did when they created their BOOK OF THE COMING FORTH BY DAY AND BY NIGHT in the Mysteries System of the Nile Valley and Great Lakes Regions of Alkebu-lan [Africa]. It is a distinct command to African People who called themselves "CHRISTIANS, JEWS" and "MOSLEMS" [or "MUSLIMS"] to write their own VERSIONS of everything affecting their every aspect of human endeavour and religious aspiration.

If we ever had any NEED FOR A BLACK BIBLE the above examples removed all doubts. If they did not, it is because we are conditioned in our European and European-American shadow mentality much deeper than we suspected for centuries; which only indicates the extent that we have been damaged by MENTAL SLAVERY imposed upon us by our slavemasters. There is more than ample reason for THE NEED FOR A BLACK BIBLE, which will be detailed in the following text of this work THE BLACK MAN'S RELIGION, Volume III.

ADDED BIBLIOGRAPHY USED IN THE LECTURES AND NOT CITED WITHIN THE TEXTS
[Chronologically listed according to use only]

H.W. Smith, MAN AND HIS GODS, Boston, Mass.,
J. Hastings [ed], ENCYCLOPAEDIA OF RELIGION AND ETHICS, New York, 1908 [13 vols.]
Sir J. Frazier, THE GOLDEN BOUGH, London, 1911 [13 vols.]
Dr. A. Churchward, THE ORIGIN AND EVOLUTION OF RELIGION, London, 1924
----------- SIGNS AND SYMBOLS OF PRIMODIAL MAN, New York, 1928
----------- ORIGIN AND EVOLUTION OF THE HUMAN RACE, London, 1920
Sir J. Frazier, FOLK-LORE IN THE OLD TESTAMENT, New York, 1923
J. H. Breastead, DEVELOPMENT OF RELIGION AND THOUGHT IN ANCIENT EGYPT, Gloucester, Mass., 1970 [3 vols.]
Theo H. Gaster, MYTH, LEGEND, AND CUSTOM IN THE OLD TESTAMENT, New York, 1969
Sir E.A. Wallis Budge, THE GODS OF THE EGYPTIAN, Chicago, Ill., 1904 [2 vols.]
Isaac Myer, QABBALAH, The Philosophical Writings Of Avicerbron, Philadelphia, Pa., 1888
Dr. J.H. Hertz [ed], THE PENTATEUCH and HAFTORAHS, U.S.A. [date unknown, 2 vols.]
J.H. Breastead, THE DAWN OF CONCIENCE, New York, 1934
Sir E.A. Wallis Budge, TALISMAN AND AMULETS, New York
A. S. Rapporport, MYTH AND LEGEND OF ANCIENT ISRAEL, New York, 1966 [2 vols.]
J. Gardiner, THE ATTITUDE OF THE ANCIENT EGYPTIANS TO DEATH AND THE DEAD, Cambridge, England, 1935
R. Graves, THE GREEK MYTHS, Baltimore, Maryland, 1905 [2 vols.]
Henri Frankfort, ANCIENT EGYPTIANS RELIGION, New York, 1948
--------- KINGSHIP AND THE GODS, Chicago, Ill., 1928
H.S. Robinson and K. Wilson, THE ENCYCLOPAEDIA OF MYTHS AND LEGENDS OF ALL NATIONS, London, 1962
E.O. James, MYTH AND RITUAL IN THE ANCIENT NEAR EAST, London, 1958
S.N. Kramer [ed.], MYTHOLOGIES OF THE ANCIENT WORLD, Garden City, N.Y., 1961
Andrew Lang, MYTH, RITUAL AND RELIGION, London, 1913 [2 vols.]
Theophile J. Meek, HEBREW ORIGINS, New York, 1936
K. Thomas, RELIGION AND THE DECLINE OF MAGIC, New York, 1971
E. and M.A. Radford, ENCYCLOPAEDIA OF SUPERSTITIONS, London, 1948
J. Trachtenberg, JEWISH MAGIC AND SUPERSTITION: A STUDY IN FOLK RELIGION, Philadelphia, Pa., and Cleveland, Ohio, 1939
J.A. Wilson, THE INTELLECTUAL ADVENTURE OF ANCIENT MAN, Chicago, Ill., 1946
E. Amati, PALESTINE BEFORE THE HEBREWS, New York, 1962
Sir A. Keith, NEW DISCOVERIES RELATING TO THE ANTIQUITY OF MAN, London, 1948
T.D. McCown and Sir A. Keith, THE STONE AGE OF MOUNT CARMEL, London, 1939
G. Maspero, HISTORY OF EGYPT, London, 1880 [13 vols.]
-------- LIFE IN ANCIENT EGYPT AND ASSYRIA, New York, 1895 [2 vols.]
-------- THE DAWN OF CIVILIZATION, EGYPT AND CHALDEA, London, 1901
Wm. Palmer, EGYPTIAN CHRONICLES, London, 1861 [2 vols.]
J.H. Breasted, ANCIENT RECORDS OF EGYPT: HISTORICAL DOCUMENTS, Chicago, Ill., 1906 [4 vols.]
G. Massey, ANCIENT EGYPT THE LIGHT OF THE WORLD, New York, 1907
Sir E.A. Wallis Budge, A HISTORY OF EGYPT, London, 1902 [4 vols.]
G. Steindorff and K.C. Seele, WHEN EGYPT RULED THE EAST, Chicago, Ill., 1942
W.M. Flanders Petrie, THE ROYAL TOMBS OF THE FIRST DYNASTY, London, 1901
A. Erman, THE LITERATURE OF THE ANCIENT EGYPTIANS [translated into English by A.M. Blackman], London, 1927

[Added bibliography continued from page 65]

T.E. Peet, A COMPARATIVE STUDY OF THE LITERATURES OF EGYPT, PALESTINE, AND MESOPOTAMIA, London, 1931
J.J. Williams, HEBREWISM OF WEST AFRICA, New York, 1930
J.G. Jackson, INTRODUCTION TO AFRICAN CIVILIZATION, New York, 1970
C. Williams, DESTRUCTION OF AFRICAN CIVILIZATION, New York, 1970
J.C. deGraft-Johnson, AFRICAN GLORY, London, 1945
R.J. Braidwood, PREHISTORIC MEN, Chicago, Ill., 1948
M.C. Burkitt, THE OLD STONE AGE, New York, 1949 [2nd ed.]
V.G. Childe, THE DAWN OF EUROPEAN CIVILIZATION, New York, 1948 [4th ed.]
------ NEW LIGHT ON THE MOST OF THE ANCIENT EAST, New York, 1934
C.S. Coon, THE ORIGIN OF RACES, New York, 1962
---- THE RACES OF EUROPE, New York, 1939
E.A. Hooten, UP FROM THE APE, New York, 1946 [Rev. ed.]
W. Houalls, MANKIND SO FAR, New York, 1945
P. Radin, PRIMITIVE RELIGION, New York, 1937
J. Vendryes, LANGUAGE, A LINGUISTIC INTRODUCTION TO HISTORY, [as translated by P. Radin], New York, 1931
F. Weidenrich, APES, GIANTS AND MEN, Chicago, Ill., 1946
Henri Frankfort, et al., BEFORE PHILOSOPHY, New York, 1949
------------- INTELLECTUAL ADVENTURE OF ANCIENT MAN, Chicago, Ill., 1946
C.J. Gadd, HISTORY AND MONUMENTS OF Ur, New York, 1929
I.E.S. Edwards, THE PYRAMIDS OF EGYPT, New York, 1947
S.R.K. Glanville, THE EGYPTIANS, London, 1933
H.E. Winlock, THE RISE AND FALL OF THE MIDDLE KINGDOM IN THEBES, New York, 1947
W.F. Albright, FROM STONE AGE TO CHRISTIANITY, Baltimore, Maryland, 1940
A. Bertholet, A HISTORY OF HEBREW CIVILIZATION, [translated by A.K. Dallas], London, 1926
E.R. Bevan and C. Singer, THE LEGACY OF ISRAEL, Oxford, 1927
L. Delaporte, THE HITTITES, Paris, 1936
O.R. Gurney, THE HITTITES, Harmondsworth, 1964
G.F. Moore, HISTORY OF RELIGIONS, New York, 1936
I. Mendelsohn, SLAVERY IN THE ANCIENT NEAR EAST, New York, 1949
A.T. Olmstead, A HISTORY OF THE PERSIAN EMPIRE, Chicago, Ill., 1948
R.W. Rogers, A HISTORY OF ANCIENT PERSIA, New York, 1929
P.A. Sykes, A HISTORY OF PERSIA, London, 1930 [2 vols., 3rd. ed.]
G.L. Huxley, ACHAEANS AND HITTITES, Oxford, 1960

Thou was not born for death, immortal bird!
No hungry generations tread thee down;
The voice I hear this passing night was heard
In ancient days by emperor and clown....[1]

---

1. I close with this extract from Keat's ODE TO A NIGHTINGALE.

Rear cover designed by Y. ben-Jochannan - from the "Judgment Scene" in the Book Of The Dead and Papyrus Of Ani, showing "THE WEIGHING OF ANI'S HEART AGAINST THE FEATHER OF LIFE."

SUNDAY NEWS, October 7, 1973

Spain's Black Madonna Venerated for Years

By BEN CARRUTHERS

The shrine of the Black Madonna, high in the vastness of Montserrat, the Serrated Mountain of northeastern Spain, has been a favored destination for Christian pilgrims for centuries. Discovered in the 11th century during the peninsula's occupation by the Moors, the stooped black figure holding her Son on her knees has been venerated by popes and popes-to-be (the latest was John XXIII), emperors, kings and queens, nobles and hordes of the common people of nearly every race and nationality.

The Black Madonna is the patroness of Catalonia and is enshrined in a chapel on a natural shelf in the highest of the sawtoothed mountains, a mere 40 miles northwest of Barcelona.

The shrine is easily reached by road or rail from the metropolis and few are the occasions when the visitor does not witness a Catalonian wedding, confirmation or christening in the chapel.

The jagged peaks of Montserrat rise abruptly 4,000 feet from the Catalonian plain and were formed eons ago, according to geologists, by a cataclysmic upsurge of volcanic rock. Legend has it that it was from these heights that Satan tempted Jesus with the riches of this world.

NEWS photo by Jack Clarity

Replica of famed statue of Black Madonna and Child is admired by Ben Carruthers, secretary of Society of American Travel Writers.

A steep road from the base of the mountain leads upward to a flat indentation at the 2,900-foot level where the shrine itself is built, but one may also take a cable car this far and a second to the crest of the mountain where monasteries of silent Trappist orders have been in existence as long as the Virgin's shrine itself.

Trappist Monasteries

The chapel on the first level is, of course, the focal point of pilgrimage. Medieval in style, it is spacious, richly appointed and enhanced by the a capella voices of 400 adolescent boys whose range is from high soprano to bass. The Black Madonna and Child sit enclosed in crystal above the high altar and may be approached by means of a marble staircase leading from the right aisle.

The statue's origin has long been shrouded in mystery. One account has it that the image was carved by St. Luke the Apostle and hidden in a cave on the mountainside until found in the Middle Ages. Another story would have us believe that the faces and hands of Mother and Son were blackened by the smoke from thousands of tallow candles burned before them over the centuries, but for me there is a much more logical explanation.

This is that the images were carved by a Moorish Christian during the long centuries of Moorish occupation of Iberia which began in 711 and, by 732, had swept across the entire peninsula and into France as far as Tours.

Because of the Koran's prohibition of prejudice based on color, many blacks from prince to slave were enlisted in the Moslem conquerors' ranks. We know, too, that many of the African occupiers were converted to Christianity long before Ferdinand and Isabella, having completed the Reconquest, exiled Moors and Jews who refused to become Christians in order to unify the country's religion as well as its political structure.

At Montserrat the Virgin and Child were carved in wood to half normal size and richly robed in medieval costume. The Madonna is seated on a simple straight-backed chair holding the Child on both knees. Robed in gold, the two figures are crowned while the Madonna is also mantled in red, white, blue and gold. The Child holds an orb in His left hand while He raises His right in a gesture of benediction. His Mother holds a larger orb in her right hand while the left arm curves protectingly around Her Son. The Virgin's features are sharp, the Son's much less so but faces, hands and Jesus' bare feet are burnished ebony while His hair, visible under the crown, is very curly.

Historical fact attests the finding of the double statue in the eleventh century, but here again legend intervenes to the effect that when authorities sought to bring it down the mountain, the figure grew heavier so that ecclesiastic authorities decided that the images did not wish to leave Montserrat and ordered them restored to that sanctuary.

Today's visitor to Montserrat will find an enormous complex of modern buildings surrounding the shrine itself. There are, of course, Benedictine monasteries, since it is that order which has jurisdiction and the monks' brew, an elexir reminiscent of French Benedictine liqueur. There are also hotels, dining rooms, refectories, souvenir stalls and even a post-office.

To visit Montserrat on a sunny day brings a lift to one's spirits regardless of his religion and, as he gazes above at the enormous rock jagged formations on the crest above the shrine itself, he can understand the awe in which this place is held.

Indeed, its mood changes rapidly according to the weather and, though I have never had the experience, I should welcome the opportunity of visiting Montserrat during a storm! Surely Wagner could have chosen no more suitable spot than "Montsalvat" (his version of Montserrat) for "Parsifal," his great religious music drama of the Holy Grail.

Taking advantage of the religious cliche, " AS FAITH WOULD HAVE IT, " this most timely article came at the completion of the next to last editorial work of this manuscript. It fits completely into the pattern of documentation I have been revealing from the time I wrote my first book in 1938 C.E. But I had to ask myself: Why did the author of this article failed to show that this "BLACK MADONNA" AND CHILD is just another of the hundreds that were once very common throughout all of so-called "CHRISTIAN EUROPE" and "GREAT BRITAIN" before 'WHITE RACISM' became part of the basic foundatian of "MODERN EUROPEAN CHRISTENDOM;" all of which has been equally transfered to 'EUROPEAN [white] AMERICA.'

He failed to point out that hundreds of years before the FIRST of the "MOORS"..."CONVERSION TO CHRISTIANITY...," from the beginning of their conquest and colonial occupation of the entire IBERIAN PENINSULA [Spain, Portugal and Southern France] in ca. 711 [or 712] C.E. up to their final expulsion from said power in ca. 1485 C.E. at Granada, Spain, their fellow indigenous "BLACK" [African] PEOPLE of North and Northeast AFRICA [Alkebu-lan] had already created and developed the THEOSOPHY, THEOLOGY and PHILOSOPHY that were later on to be condensed into the term "CHRISTIANITY." For it was in "EGYPT"[Ta-Merry, Kamt, etc.], "NUBIA" [Ta-Nehisi, Zeti, etc.] and "ETHIOPIA" [Itiopi, Abyssinia, etc.] Boetius, Pantaeus and others started this "RELIGIOUS INSTITUTION" called "CHRISTENDOM." In this same context one must remember that "ETHIOPIA" was a "CHRISTIAN NATION" - officially - for over ONE HUNDRED AND TWENTY-FOUR YEARS before Constantine "the great" took the Throne Of The Roman Empire in 312 C.E. and made Rome a "CHRISTIAN NATION" - officially.

Have we forgotten that there were SEVEN PATRIARCHS [Popes] and TWENTY-FOUR BISHOPS of the "NEW RELIGION" or "CHRISTIANITY" in North, Northeast and Northwest AFRICA before the FIRST ONE in all of EUROPE, including ROME? Also, that the most prolific and fundamental works on CHRISTIAN MORALS and ETHICS still in use by "CHRISTIANS" were written by three BLACK [African] CHRISTIAN CHURCH FATHERS: Tertullian, [St.] Cyprian and [St.] Augustine [see AFRICAN ORIGINS OF THE MAJOR "WESTERN RELIGIONS: JUDAISM, CHRISTIANITY AND ISLAM, Volume I, Chapter TWO].

It is indeed very sad that the "BLACK" color of JESUS "the Christ" OF NAZARETH had to be made LILY-WHITE before "modern" European and European-American so-called "CHRISTIANS" could have accepted HIS HUMANITY and final DIVINITY. Maybe it will be further reveal that the entire concept of the "BLACK MADONNA AND CHILD" sprung from another story of "BLACK" [African] PEOPLE - the Goddess ISIS and her Virgin Birth Son - the God HORUS, both having comprise what is known as the "GODDESS OF FERTILITY AND CHILD" symbol of an origin of no less than ca. 4100 B.C.E. [see BLACK MAN OF THE NILE AND HIS FAMILY, Chapter X: "Mother Of The Gods Of Man," pp. 372 - 378].

Although the subject of the BLACK MADONNA AND CHILD is properly treated in other areas of this three volume work, the following from page 373 of BLACK MAN OF THE NILE AND HIS FAMILY is of great assistance at this juncture, and should be compared to the above article.

Chapter X: MOTHER OF THE GODS OF MAN

MOTHER AND CHILD

Middle Kingdom Period, c. 2100 - 1675 B. C. E. [Bronze H, 5"]
Berlin-Charlottenburg, Staaliche Museen der Stiftung PreuBisher Kulturbesitz, Egyptian Department.

In describing the above BLACK MADONNA AND CHILD statue the Museum writers stated that "...BOTH HAVE TYPICAL NEGROID CHARACTERISTICS...," etc.

[See Volume III, pages 26 - 38 for further details related to the entire Madonna concept, etc.]

The following quotations from AFRICAN ORIGINS OF THE MAJOR "WESTERN RELIGIONS: JUDAISM, CHRISTIANITY AND ISLAM are most appropriate at this juncture. On page 81 a quotation from Jame Soames' THE COAST OF THE BARBARY, pp. 30 - 31 reads:

> At the height of Roman power in North Africa, the population of Italy was actually declining and there was never any vast number of Roman colonists in the racial sense of the word. The Romans knew nothing of those modern emotions which are to us so powerful and omnipresent that we can hardly imagine a civilization from which they should be absent; she had neither colour prejudice nor religious intolerance in the days of the Republic. The Christian martyrs of the early church suffered because they were felt to be a menace to the State, propagating doctrines subversive to good order and discipline: they were regarded as the Communists of their day. But highly cultivated Roman opinion considered all religions to be essentially the diverse manifestations of one great truth, and had no conception of that white heat of missionizing zeal which would put whole populations of unbelievers to the sword or send men to the scaffold and the fire for the sake of a disputed theological definition.
>
> All that part of the make-up of men's minds came later, as did the acute sense of differentiation of race and consequent antagonism which may be summed up in the phrase "colour bar."

She also wrote the following about [St.] Augustine - THE BISHOP OF HIPPO REGIOUS, North Africa:

> It was in such a world, torn by civil strife and threatened by barbarian invasion under the splendid but fading shadow of Rome, that St. Augustine's genius flowered. The Church in Africa had produced great men before this day; the writings of Tertullian and St. Cyprian both testify to its keen intellectual vitality; but neither achieved his stature - the last and noblest product of Roman African civilization. We learn a great deal about that civilization from the CONFESSIONS, the product of a mentality strikingly sympathetic to the European mind, <u>though bearing the imprint of its African origin</u>.

In the next paragraph she nailed the coffin closed on WHITE RACISM and RELIGIOUS BIGOTRY in European and European-American "WHITE CHRISTIAN THEOLOGY" that is still the "ORDER OF THE DAY" in the United States of America, Great Britain and Europe. She wrote:

> St. Augustine is far more comprehensible to a European audience today than are most contemporary North African authors - a fact which is in striking disproof of modern racial theories, for it is community of philosophy which makes for affinity far more than the accident of birth.

LIST OF PHARAOHS AND QUEENS OF TA-MERRY, TA-NEHISI, MERÖE AND ITIOPI MENTIONED CHRONOLOGICALLY IN THE TEXT, ETC.

Page	Dynasty	Pharaoh's Name	Period Reigned	Place of Origin
7	XVIIIth	Haremheb  Ser-χeperu-Rā-setep-en-Rā, son of the Sun, Āmen-meri-en Ḥeru-em-heb.	1340 - 1320	Luxor or Thebes
7	XIXth	Rameses I 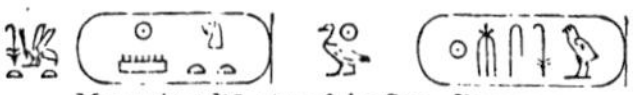 Men-peḥtet-Rā, son of the Sun, Rā-messu.	1320 - 1318	Luxor or Thebes
9	XIXth	Rameses II  Usr-māt-Rā setep-en-Rā, son of the Sun, Rā-messu-meri-Āmen.	1298 - 1232	Luxor or Thebes
10	Ist	Aha [Narmer or Menes] 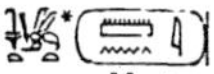 Menȧ.	3200 - 2980	Ta-Nehisı [Nubia]
13	XVIIIth	Queen Hatshepsut: The only Queen in history to have been officially listed as a Pharaoh [King];  Māt-ka-Rā, son of the Sun, Ḥāt-shepset-χnem-Āmen.	1515 - 1484	Luxor or Thebes
13	XVIIIth	Amenhotep III  Neb-māt-Rā, son of the Sun, Āmen-ḥetep ḥeq-Uast.	1370 - 1352	Luxor or Thebes
20	XXIVth	Piankhi 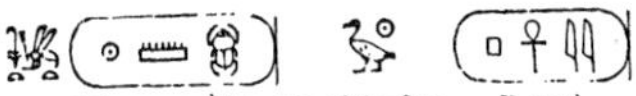 Men-χeper-Rā, son of the Sun, P-ānχi.	718 - 717	Itiopi
34	XIVth	Sexeper-em-Ra 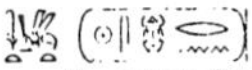 Seχeper-en-Rā.	? - 1675	Luxor or Thebes
39	XIXth	Seti I  Men-māt-Rā, son of the Sun, Ptaḥ-meri-en-Seti.	1319 - 1298	Luxor or Thebes
47	XXXth	Nectabnebus 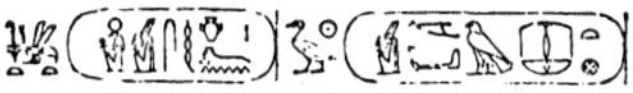 S-net'em-āb-Rā setep-en-Āmen, son of the Sun, Neχt-Ḥeru-ḥebt-meri-Āmen.	378 - 360	Luxor or Thebes

Page	Dynasty	Pharaoh's Name	Period Reigned	Place of Origin
49	IVth	Khufu [Cheops or Kheops]	2243 - 2220	Memphis
		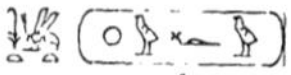 χufu.		
55	XVIIIth	Tut-ankh-Amen	? - 1349	Luxor or Thebes
		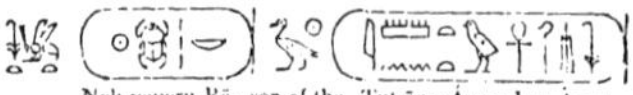 Neb-χeperu-Rā, son of the Sun, Tut-ānχ-Āmen ḥeq Ānnu resu (?)		
62	XXVIth	Necho [Neku or Nechu]	609 - 594	Sais
		 Nem-āb-Rā, son of the Sun, Nekau.		

Y. ben-Jochannan/ Al Burliegh Photo Studio, New York, N.Y./72

130219-200-36-60W